**Like and follow me on Facebook and Instagram, respectively, to see weekly posts on counseling adventures and on the latest counseling resources!**

www.schoolcounselorstephanie.com
www.facebook.com/schoolcounselorstephanie
www.instagram.com/schoolcounselorstephanie
www.pinterest.com/schoolcounselorstephanie/

youth light inc.


Published by YouthLight, Inc.

Printed in the United States of America.

ISBN: 978-1-59850-250-3
Library of Congress Control Number: 2020940169

10 9 8 7 6 5 4 3 2 1
Printed in the United States of America

**For information on this publication or others by this author, visit www.youthlight.com or e-mail the author at stephanie@schoolcounselorstephanie.com.**

# DEDICATION

***To My Mom***

*A master educator who was*
*implementing trauma-informed practices*
*long before it was the trend.*

# TABLE OF CONTENTS

# INTRODUCTION

In my career, I've been so fortunate to experience many opportunities to share my counseling strategies with professionals across the nation, and especially in Texas, where I live. In these conversations, I talk a lot about the themes interwoven throughout this book- solution focused brief counseling, general counseling practices, and trauma informed practices. Inevitably, in almost every single one of these opportunities where the word trauma is mentioned, a counselor will come up to me in the middle or after the presentation to tell me some version of, "I have two students who have suffered from trauma and they would really benefit from these strategies that you are sharing, but what do I do with the other students? The ones who haven't suffered from trauma?" And to this my response is always the same. First, I tell the counselor that they may have many more than two students who have experienced a traumatic event since trauma has a way of shaming people into silence (but that's a topic for another book). Second, I give them my heart healthy eating analogy to illustrate how trauma-informed practices benefit all students, even those who have not experienced trauma:

*Imagine a family where one member who has heart disease is advised by their doctor to start a diet consisting primarily of fruits, vegetables and whole grains; this medical advice is given in order to lessen the damage of the family member's heart disease. Even though this member is the only one in the home with heart disease, all members of the family who follow this diet will also experience health benefits. Trauma-informed interventions work in much the same way with children who have not experienced trauma (Lerner, 2018)!*

So, all of this to say that this book, *Helping in Hard Places*, is a counseling book for ALL counselors and for ALL children- whether they've suffered textbook trauma or just spent some time in a hard place of their own definition.

## Purpose of this Book & Topics Covered

*Helping in Hard Places* provides school counselors and other mental health professionals with a blueprint for infusing trauma-informed practices into their counseling interventions in a way that supports all children. The nature of trauma-informed practices is that they are needed to support children of trauma, but they are beneficial to everyone, regardless of whether they've experienced trauma or not. This is because they are composed of the most pure and needed supports that all humans can utilize to overcome adversity: such as healthy relationships, routine, repetition, a safe environment, time, and patience. For this reason, *Helping in Hard Places* will focus on supporting all children by infusing trauma-informed practices into individual counseling sessions, student support groups, and whole class lessons. This book will also incorporate many techniques from the Solution-Focused Brief Counseling (SFBC) Model since it is the best-suited counseling model for the school setting. According to Dr. Gerald Sklare, a dynamic thought-leader in the movement to infuse SFBC into schools, this counseling model is "ideally suited for schools" where caseloads are often huge and the focus is on keeping kids in the classroom to maximize learning; as a result, "counselors need a focused approach suitable for a range of problems" (Sklare, 2005, p. xi). In addition, SFBC techniques are extremely effective in bringing about positive change in students who have suffered from trauma, as well as those who have not experienced trauma. The reason for this comes from the main idea behind all solution focused brief counseling, which is that, "Students/Clients are uplifted when their strengths rather than their deficits are emphasized in the solution focused process. This provides incentives to advance their successful efforts" (Sabella, 2019, p. 5). More explanation on these ideas will be provided in the following counseling guides included in this book.

| TITLE | TOPIC |
|---|---|
| Way to Goal! | An Individual Counseling Guide |
| The Support Cohort | A Group Counseling Guide |
| Overcoming Strife in Life | A Guidance Lesson Curriculum |

# What is Trauma-Informed School Counseling & Why it is Important?

Everyone in the mental health and education worlds is talking about trauma these days and for good reason! According to the American School Counseling Association (2016), "46 million children witness violence, crime, physical and psychological abuse every year in the United States" (para. 2). The Centers for Disease Control (CDC) call these traumatic events Adverse Childhood Experiences (ACEs). The CDC (2019) states that, "Adverse Childhood Experiences have been linked to risky health behaviors, chronic health conditions, low life potential, and early death. As the number of ACEs increases, so does the risk for these outcomes" (para. 1). So, let's start with a definition of trauma from the CDC (n.d.)- they say that traumatic events involve a threat of serious injury or death and are usually experienced with a sense of terror, extreme stress, and helplessness. Fortunately, trauma-informed school counseling practices can help with this! These practices occur when counselors are able to recognize students who have been impacted by traumatic stress and then use interventions that create protective factors such as success in school, healthy relationships with peers and adults, positive coping skills, safety, clear rules, and more (Youth.gov, 2020). And in keeping with the idea that trauma-informed practices are beneficial for everyone, let's take this one step further- these protective factors create stable, safe, and nurturing environments that will benefit any child, so let's set them up for everyone!

While common sense tells us that a supportive, positive school environment is needed for any child to receive an optimal educational experience, research shows us that this environment also decreases the effects of trauma! School success (CDC, 2009) and supportive/healthy relationships with an adult/s (Perry & Szalavitz , 2017) are especially powerful protective factors that can change the lives of traumatized children. And school counselors play a key role in establishing this environment for their students. According to the American School Counselor Association (2016), this includes the following practices:

- "recognize the signs of trauma in students
- understand traumas need not predict individual failure if sufficient focus on resilience and strengths is present
- avoid practices that may re-traumatize students
- implement effective academic and behavioral practices, such as positive behavioral interventions and supports and social and emotional learning
- promote safe, stable and nurturing relationships
- provide community resource information to students and families dealing with trauma
- educate staff on the effects of trauma and how to refer students to the school counselor" (p. 66).

As you can see, most of these practices can be implemented through whole-class lessons, group sessions, and individual work, which make up the three sections of this book. Additionally, each of these three implementation modes (lesson, group, individual) are enhanced with Solution Focused Brief Counseling (SFBC) strategies! So, let's take a closer look now at SFBC and why it is a must to incorporate into your counseling practices.

# Solution-Focused Brief Counseling

Another crucial aspect of helping students in need is utilizing a goal or solution focused counseling approach. In all my years of school counseling, I have seen nothing that even comes to a close second to the Solution Focused Brief Counseling (SFBC) model in terms of effectiveness in the school setting. SFBC is THE go-to model for counseling in schools. According to Dr. John Murphy, another SFBC thought leader, "The simple and pragmatic emphasis on doing what works is a refreshing change from the more cumbersome approaches that are impractical for schools" (Murphy, 2008, viii). So, what exactly is Solution Focused Brief Counseling? Well, in explanation, I'd like to borrow the wise words of Dr. Russ Sabella, who can explain SFBC better than anyone I know.

*This model uses a systematic, five-step approach in which students/clients focus on solutions rather than problems. They are encouraged to think about times when they were performing better (exceptions), how past behavior contributed to being more on-track, and how to recreate such circumstances in their present situations. Focus is on the clients' strengths and abilities rather than their weaknesses or limitations. (Sabella, 2019, p. 4)*

The SFBC model, as it is used in schools today, is based on the work of Steve de Shazer and Insoo Kim Berg who together developed Solution-Focused Therapy (SFT) in the late 1970s. SFT proposes that clients have the solutions to their problems, even if they are yet undiscovered; "that by rediscovering their resources, clients are encouraged to repeat past successes" (Sklare, 2014, p. x). This idea, when transferred into SFBC for the school setting, is perfect for kids in need- especially those who have experienced trauma! For example, think how empowering it would be for a student to realize that they have the solution to their problem inside themselves! For another example, imagine guiding a child to change their perspective so that instead of seeing their hardship as an event that holds them back in life, they see it as an obstacle that will only make them stronger once they overcome it. And this same transformation of turning a hardship into a strengthening experience will happen with so many other SFBC strategies such as creating a self-chosen goal and then recognizing small steps toward the achievement of it (Lutz, 2018). For this reason, you will notice SFBC techniques integrated into each of my 3 book sections, individual, group, and classroom. Through effective SFBC strategies, all students, whether they've experienced trauma or not, can experience the successes that come from concentrating on solutions, rather than problems.

# Virtual Counseling

Our world turned upside down just before this book went to print. With the COVID-19 pandemic, many counselors wondered about how to facilitate individual sessions, student support groups, and whole class guidance lessons during the social distancing shutdown. And many of us started to worry most about our students of trauma. After all, we know how much our traumatized students struggle in normal times. Therefore, it stands to reason that these students will face even greater hardships in this scary and stressful pandemic reality that we are all living now! So, you might be thinking, what do I do to help my struggling and traumatized students through virtual counseling? Well, let's talk about that. Even though the sessions and activities were created before the homebound learning tsunami hit, most of them can be easily modified for the online learning and tele-counseling settings. I've added a distance learning piece to each of the three recommendations sections in this book to give you tips and resources for how to modify your sessions/lessons for the online environment. More than ever, all your students can benefit from these trauma-informed sessions since living through a pandemic is, well… traumatic. We are definitely finding ourselves in some strange times these days. As counselors and educators, we serve as a voice of hope and reason when the world is in disarray around us. And I commend you all on doing the most amazing job at this hard, hard work. However, it takes its toll on us...after all, despite being superheroes, we are still human. But the good news is that one day we will get to the "After" of this pandemic chaos.

So, let's dive right into all the ways that counselors can support students and establish protective factors through the three main avenues of the counseling delivery system: individual counseling sessions, student support groups, and whole-class lessons.

# WAY TO GOAL!
# An Individual Counseling Guide

***A calmer, healthier mind seemed like a good place to start reversing  the effects of toxic stress.***

Dr. Nadine Burke Harris, *The Deepest Well*

## Flora's Story

Many years ago, I had the enlightening experience of counseling a student who was adamant that she did not want to talk to a therapist. Even though she was very good at talking, she did not want to be referred out for talk therapy. Let's call her Flora. Flora had been removed from her biological parents at a young age due to abuse and was living with her guardians; she was plagued by issues of abandonment and traumatic grief. I had seen her respond really favorably to counseling through goal work, but she needed a more intensive version of it than I, as a school counselor, could provide. Her aversion to traditional therapy required me to search for other supports for her, such as art therapy or animal therapy. We did some research together and I discovered her love of horses so we settled on Equine Assisted Psychotherapy (EAP). She was excited, and we set a goal for her to get some kind of counseling help through EAP. I reached out to her guardian and we scheduled her for some local EAP sessions. The day after her first EAP session, she came bouncing into my office to excitedly tell me about how a horse that had recently lost her baby "chose" Flora to be her partner because Flora had lost her own mother. Her success with counseling through this alternative therapy was breathtaking. Within just a few months, she was more positive, her grades had improved, and she frequently wanted to update me on her work (and further goals) with the horses. The following year, she even got a horse of her own. Years later, I ran into her at a local bakery and she told me all about her continued success through riding and interacting with horses.

So, I tell you Flora's story to highlight the importance of goal work in trauma-informed counseling. Guiding a child to a goal that is relevant to them is life-changing, whether they suffer from trauma or not. In addition to goal work, strategies such as self-esteem strengtheners, and coping skills help to establish protective factors for children. And so many of these types of strategies fall under the umbrella of solution-focused brief counseling, which you will notice throughout Way to Goal. These practices "buffer the adverse effects of trauma and its stressful aftermath" (NCTSN, 2012, p. 3). Moreover, establishing a supportive and nurturing relationship with an adult (or even a horse) is key. According to Dr. Bruce Perry (2017) of the Child Trauma Academy, "what works best is anything that increases the quality and number of relationships in a child's life" (p. 85). Dr. Perry goes on to say that one of the greatest lessons that he's learned in his work with children is, "the importance of simply taking the time, before doing anything else, to pay attention and listen" (p. 274). Accordingly, it is only through that initial careful attention, that a counselor can optimally help the child to develop a goal that is meaningful to them. As you can imagine, the individual counseling session is a particularly effective place to implement these trauma-informed interventions.

# Recommendations for Facilitating Individual Counseling

## *Starting Individual Sessions*

- Meet once per week for 30 minutes to 1 hour in a quiet, private room or area. Teenagers can meet for the full hour, elementary-aged kids will max out at 30 minutes. Alternatively, you can meet with some students once every two weeks- this works best with organized, mature students who will self-practice.
- After this recommendations section, a plan for each session is provided with the accompanying reproducible worksheets and resources needed for that session. At the end of the individual counseling guide, additional activities and data templates are compiled for easy reference.
- This guide has various, leveled resources, making it appropriate for use with children in grades 3 through high school.
- This individual counseling guide was developed for use in a school setting, but it can easily be modified for use in a clinical or even virtual setting.
- These session plans can be easily adapted for the virtual school counseling setting by following the activity steps on a FERPA-compliant online platform such as Zoom or Google Classroom. Google has a tutorial with directions on how to set up Google Hangouts Meet so you can meet with the student. Take some time to set it up and then practice using it with a family member or a colleague first, just so you have it down. Additionally, written work such as goal note cards, interest forms, scaling sheets, pre/posttests, and final evaluations can be done through an online comments, Q&A features, or simply by having members show or email their responses to you.
- Set up your weekly sessions to end after 4 sessions with a plan to evaluate and discuss with the student if more is needed after the last session. Since the school environment is generally not the appropriate environment for long-term therapy, it is best to refer out to a licensed mental health care professional if the child needs more support than short-term individual counseling can provide (ASCA, 2016). Keep in mind that this is a psychoeducational sessions guide. It should be used to educate students on mental health and wellness information and strategies. It should not be used as a substitute for mental health therapy with a licensed practitioner.
- It is important to screen students for inclusion in recurring sessions of individual counseling. If the child can be best served through short-term, recurring individual counseling sessions (rather than group sessions or whole class lessons), proceed by determining if the student meets the data-based criteria that must be met in order to be enrolled in recurring individual counseling. According the American School Counseling Association (2016), it is important to have defined expectations for the students in counseling and that these expectations should be based on data. Therefore, when a student is referred to you for short-term individual counseling (i.e., by parent, student self-referral, or staff member), check that student's data against your school counseling program's data-based criteria that students must meet in order to be enrolled in individual counseling. Below is an example of these types of criteria.

***POSSIBLE DATA-BASED CRITERIA FOR RECURRING INDIVIDUAL COUNSELING:***

**Individual Criteria #1: Student is failing at least 2 classes.**

AND/OR

**Individual Criteria #2: Student has at least one In School Suspension referral.**

AND/OR

**Individual Criteria #3: Student has had at least 1 crisis/emergency incident.**

- It is also important to orient the student to the individual counseling experience. So, once you have determined that a student meets the criteria, meet briefly with them to discuss the topic/purpose of the counseling, obtain verbal informed assent and discuss the limits of confidentiality (ASCA, 2016). Use the following for guidance in discussing assent and confidentiality:
  - > Does the child think it will be helpful to meet with you for individual counseling?
  - > You can use the session one "3 Hurts" Emergency reproducible for help with the limits of confidentiality.

- If the child is interested in participating, give them the permission form located in session one, so they can take it home for their parent/guardian to sign and return it to you. Then, throughout the individual counseling experience, work with the child on whatever criteria got them into counseling (possibly through goal setting/achievement).

- Plan each session using the session one Individual Counseling Notes Form.

- Keep an Individual Counseling Sessions Binder with a section for each student. In a specific student's section, keep their Individual Counseling Notes Form, student schedules/teachers (if applicable), permission form, and any handouts you will use.

## ***Running Individual Sessions***

- Individual counseling can be difficult mental work for the student, so it is important to repeat questions and experiences, give lots of thinking time, and praise them often for this strenuous work. Keep in mind that, "The brain changes in response to patterned, repetitive experiences: the more you repeat something, the more ingrained it becomes…[this means] time and patience is called for as these repetitions continue" (Perry, 2017, p. 275).

- Above all, counseling should be a positive experience, so incorporate some fun and humor into sessions whenever possible. The key is to keep the child coming back for more, while you teach them the tools to handle life's challenges on their own.

- It is good to give session homework so students can apply the skills they have learned and practiced. Application is an effective way to transfer information from short-term memory into long-term memory, where we want the child to keep their session skills. Also, utilizing the homework feature and following up with it in subsequent sessions helps to ensure that the skills learned in each session are reviewed and discussed in multiple sessions, rather than just covered in a single session. In the spirit of keeping things fun and positive, consider offering a prize if the student does their session homework.

- In some cases, it may be needed to give children a tangible short-term solution that they can use if they come to you in the initial session with a specific issue that needs immediate resolving. Of course, solving complex problems and changing behavior takes time through multiple sessions; however, it is optimal to provide an immediate tool when a student arrives to that first session with a specific problem. For example, if I am working with a student who struggles with test anxiety, during our initial session, I will provide a resource on stress reduction strategies and then briefly role-play them with the student. This short-term tool will be provided in addition to the longer process of identifying solutions and achieving goals related to their stressors.

- After every session, it is really helpful to send the student a brief reminder note to celebrate their success and remind them of their goal and counseling homework from their most recent session. The simplest way to create this note is to make a photocopy of their note card goal and then add a few sentences of your own such as:
  - > A positive comment about something they did/discussed in the session
  - > The session homework assignment
  - > A possible next step in achieving their goal

- Sometimes students are resistant to counseling. A small percentage of the general population students are so aversive to counseling or working with adults that you may really have to stretch the solution-focused brief counseling model to meet them where they are- but it is possible! There are helpful and specific techniques for working with resistant clients. Here are my favorites.

    1. Try responding to initial session resistance with a cheerful attitude of "well, we have to be here together for this half hour, so let's just make the best of it" and see what happens. Sometimes that is all it takes to power through the student's initial resistance bluff and start the real work. In these cases, have a selection of games and let the student choose one while you frame the session as "let's just play a game to get through it". It may take a couple of these types of sessions to build the trust and rapport needed counsel.

    2. Use some gentle but direct questioning to explore the reason for their resistance. For example:
        - It seems like meeting with me makes you uncomfortable, can you tell me about that?
        - You say you don't want to have counseling, can you help me understand why?
        - Tell me what you don't like about coming here to talk with me so we can find a way to work around what you don't like.

        Once you know their reasons, it is time to get creative! How can you work around what they don't like or what makes them uncomfortable? This is also a time to consult with other mental health professionals to find out what creative solutions they have used in similar situations.

    3. Decide on a solution together with the student. This solution may be achieved through counseling modifications or even compromises (partner work, pre-session reminders, shortened sessions, etc.)

    4. If they are not ready for individual counseling (i.e., a trauma just occurred in their life), consider another type of support structure such as mentoring or a non-talk counseling modality such as biblio-counseling or art counseling.

    5. Refer out. Sometimes a student is resistant to counseling because their issue is just too big for the school setting. In this case, provide the student and family with a list of clinical mental health professionals.

## *Ending Individual Sessions*

- Endings can be hard for anyone, and for the child who has experienced trauma, it may be especially tough. The best way to handle endings with a student is to be direct, and let them know that the ending is coming (details on this in session 4). In the spirit of SFBC work, frame or reframe the ending as a positive- emphasizing what is good about endings and how far the student has come; praise is also key here.

- As you can imagine, students sometimes get upset in counseling sessions, so it is important to make time and have a plan to calm things down before sending them back out into the world (especially if that world is the classroom). To facilitate this plan, have a board game ready to go that you can play for about 10 minutes before the end of the session if the student needs time and a distraction to stabilize emotions.

- Collecting data is an important part of evaluating student progress in relation to individual counseling interventions. In addition, data will help you to improve your future counseling sessions as well as promote your program with parents, administrators, staff, etc. For these reasons, I've included an extensive data plan, located after session 4 that allows you to compile, analyze, and present all aspects of your session successes to counseling program stakeholders. It is best to compile the data about 1 month after the sessions end in order to have some 'after session' data.

- During the last session, it is a good idea to make several photocopies of the student's goal note card so that you can send out a goal note reminder to the student every week for the rest of the semester with a short, personalized note. This is much like the reminder note sent during session work, and likewise helps the student to stay focused on achieving their goals after their session work with you is finished.

- Consider having a follow-up session about a month or two after counseling has ended in order to check in on a student's progress. Below are the steps to facilitate follow-up sessions.

    1. Ask student to *scale their time/experiences since the sessions ended. Ask them to explain why they have chosen this scaling number.
       ** "Scaling questions serve many purposes in solution-focused counseling, one of which is to evaluate outcomes. Students and others can be asked the following question on a regular basis throughout the counseling process: 'On a scale of 1 to 10, with 1 being the worst it can be and 10 being the best it can be, how would you rate the school problem/goal during the past week?" (Murphy, 2008, p. 78).*

    2. Take a moment to discuss with the student any issues or recent problems occurring in their life.

    3. Review the student's goal from their last session and discuss any progress made towards it. If applicable, role play and/or guide the student in creating an additional goal.

    4. Remind the student of the procedures on how they can talk with you in the future, if needed.

- I have included suggestions for additional activities (included after session 4) if you'd like to extend a session's length or have more than four sessions.

- If you would like to learn more about any of the strategies or activities in this individual counseling guide, please refer to the professional sources listed in the references section at the end of this book.

# American School Counselor Association
# STANDARDS ALIGNMENT

The American School Counselor Association (ASCA) sets the national framework for a model school counseling program. As a result, the Way to Goal sessions activities are aligned with the following ASCA Mindsets & Behaviors that can be applied to the domains of Academic Development and Personal/Social Development.

**MINDSETS**

| | |
|---|---|
| M 1. | Belief in development of whole self, including a healthy balance of mental, social/emotional and physical well-being |
| M 6. | Positive attitude toward work and learning |

**BEHAVIORS**

| | |
|---|---|
| B-SMS 1. | Demonstrate ability to assume responsibility |
| B-SMS 5. | Demonstrate perseverance to achieve long- and short-term goals |
| B-SMS 6. | Demonstrate ability to overcome barriers to learning |
| B-SMS 7. | Demonstrate effective coping skills when faced with a problem |
| B-SS 8. | Demonstrate advocacy skills and ability to assert self, when necessary |
| B-SMS 9. | Demonstrate personal safety skills |
| B-SMS 10. | Demonstrate ability to manage transitions and ability to adapt to changing situations and responsibilities |

(ASCA, 2019, p.3)

# SESSION 1 Building Rapport & Identifying Problem Areas

## TOPIC OVERVIEW

**The student will:**

- Begin relationship building with counselor
- Explore the problem that necessitates counseling work
- Start establishing the solution for counseling work

**Materials**

- Reproducibles (attached at the end of this session):
  - > Parent/Guardian Permission Letter
  - > Initial Individual Counseling Notes Form
  - > Interest Form
  - > The "3 Hurts" Emergency (should be displayed prominently in counseling area)
  - > My Scales
  - > SFBC Questioning Guide
- Pencil
- Note card

**Procedures**

1. **Introduction**
   - Begin the rapport-building process with the student by introducing yourself and having them complete the attached Interest Form. Tell the student that the purpose of the Interest Form is for you to be able to plan sessions tailored specifically for their interests and strengths.
   - Have the student share their Interest Form responses with you or ask them a few open-ended questions about their responses. Establish some commonalities and start *cheerleading, if possible. *Cheerleading is "supporting and encouraging student's success with praise" (Sklare, 2014, p. 58).
   - Briefly review the purpose of the counseling session and the general reason they were referred to you.
   - Explain the limits of confidentiality by showing the "3 Hurts" Emergency. Let the student know that every adult in the school building must work with another adult/s if students tell them of a "3 hurts" emergency; this is because the top priority is to keep students safe.
   - At this point, ask the student if they have any questions and if they are ready to proceed with the session.
2. **Problem Identification**
   - Begin by asking the student, "In your opinion, what is the reason you are here?" and "What can we do to make things better for you?"
   - Give the student the attached My Scales sheet and go over the directions with them. Explain to the student what scaling is (choosing a number on a 1-10 scale, where 10 is the best, to evaluate something) and tell them that usually we will scale verbally, but today they will start off with a paper scale. Have them complete all 3 scales on the sheet.
   - Review how the student has rated each aspect of their life on the My Scales sheet. Next, have them select which part they want to work on first in the counseling sessions; this is their "problem."
   - In order to learn more about their problem as they experience it, discuss some of the step two questions in the attached SFBC Questioning Sheet.

# Building Rapport & Identifying Problem Areas

**Procedures** *(continued)*

3. **Goal Work**
   - Explain to the student that the focus of our sessions will be on goal work because achieving goals increases student success and promotes positive mental health, no matter what previous challenges they have faced in their life (Sobhy & Cavallero, 2010).
   - Review the problem that was discussed in Step 2 above. Discuss with the student what type of goal or solution might help them solve that problem. Help them to create a tentative goal to solve the problem (it doesn't have to be a SMART goal at this point as this is just their preliminary goal to get them thinking about goal work). Write the student's tentative goal in the appropriate section of the attached Initial Individual Counseling Notes Form and on a note card for the student to take with them.
   - If student has no idea of a goal, ask Dr. John Murphy's Futureland goal question, "Pretend that you are flying in a spaceship to a planet called Futureland, where you can live your life without this problem. Describe what your life is like at school in Futureland" (2008, p. 101). You can also try the "Million Dollar Question" from the SFBC Questioning Sheet. Turn the student's answer to this question into a preliminary goal (i.e., "In Future land, no one ever yells at me to stop blurting out answers." → "So, let's talk about a goal like raising your hand to give answers, so no one will yell at you."
   - Tell the student to think about turning this tentative goal into a specific one for the next session–how will they know when they achieve it? Is it even possible to achieve? Is it important to them? How long will it take them to achieve it? Tell the student that this is their counseling homework that will be discussed at the next session.

4. **Wrap Up**
   - Praise the student! Point out successes such as answering challenging questions. Let the student know that you will continue working together on their goal in the next session.
   - Ask the student if there is anything more they would like to discuss or need help with for this week.
   - Send the student their reminder note (explained in recommendation section) on the following day.

# Parent/Guardian Permission Letter

Date: ____________________

Dear Parent/Guardian:

The Counseling Program at ________________________________ School includes individual counseling sessions. Your child ________________________________, has been referred for participation in short-term individual counseling. With your permission, your child will attend individual counseling sessions on a scheduled basis at school by the counselor. These sessions will focus on the topic of ________________________________ __________________________. The sessions will not change the child's academic program. Participation in the sessions is voluntary, and confidentiality will be discussed and respected.

At times, the counselor and school-based staff (principal, assistant principal, social worker, psychologist, behavior specialist, teacher, nurse, etc.) will need to exchange information about your child (goals, strategies, etc.). All communication will take place only on an educational need-to-know basis.

This permission is for the school year ______.

If you would like for your child to have individual counseling sessions with the counselor, please sign and return this form to the counseling office. If you have any questions or concerns, please call ________________________.

Thank you,

________________________________________________________

Counselor

I give permission for ____________________________________ to participate in individual counseling sessions.

________________________________________________

Parent/Guardian Signature

________________________________________________

Phone Number

# Initial Individual Counseling Notes Form

*Counselor Information Sheet*

Name ________________________________ **SESSION # 1** Date ____________________

> Student's Goal (It doesn't have to be SMART since it is just a tentative goal at this point.)

> Session Activities:

> Session Summary Notes:

# Interest Form

*Student Reproducible*

*The purpose of this form is for the counselor to get to know you a little better, so that they can plan your sessions in the most interesting and helpful way for you. Please answer the questions below in as much detail as possible. Alternatively, you can dictate your answers to the counselor who will write them down below.*

Name ______________________________ Date ______________

1. My favorite thing to do is ______________________________.

2. I really enjoy this part of the school day: ______________________________.

3. I really do not enjoy this part of the school day: ______________________________.

4. The best thing about my family is ______________________________

   ______________________________.

5. The best thing about me is ______________________________.

6. Something that I really struggle with is ______________________________

   ______________________________.

7. Something that I have never tried but want to experience is ______________________________

   ______________________________.

8. The job/career I want to have in my future is ______________________________.

# The "3 Hurts" Emergency

*Student Reproducible*

**An emergency is a serious situation where someone could get physically hurt!**

If you tell me about an emergency, I may have to tell another adult to keep you or someone else safe. An emergency usually involves one or more of the following "3 Hurts" situations:

**1.**
**You might physically harm YOURSELF.**

**2.**
**You might physically harm ANOTHER PERSON.**

**3.**
**SOMEONE ELSE threatens or physically harms you** *(or another person)*.

**If you have one of these "3 Hurts," tell me or another trusted adult immediately.**

# My Scales

*Student Reproducible*

*Directions: Circle the number below to show where you are (1-feeling unhappy to 10-feeling very happy) in the following three areas of your life.*

## SCHOOL

 **1 2 3 4 5 6 7 8 9 10** 

## HOME LIFE

 **1 2 3 4 5 6 7 8 9 10** 

## ME, MYSELF, AND I

 **1 2 3 4 5 6 7 8 9 10** 

# SFBC Questioning Guide

*Counselor Information & Instruction Sheet*

*Solution-focused brief counseling (SFBC) uses several different tasks to help a student to find their solution and achieve success (Murphy, 2008). I have created questions that the counselor can use to help guide a student to their solution/s or goal/s. These questions are grouped into my own 5 stages below.*

1. **Building Student-Counselor Relationship**
   - Tell me about the best part of your day or week.
   - What is something you'd like me to know about you?
   - What do you want to be when you grow up? (Can link to problem and goal.)
   - How do you feel about starting counseling today?

2. **The Problem**
   - Tell me about a problem in your life.
   - If I could watch your problem on my phone, what would I see?
   - What are the 5Ws of the problem (who, what, where, when, why)?
   - Tell me about previous counseling you've had.

3. **Creating a Goal**
   - What would you like to do to change this problem?
   - Million Dollar Question: If someone would give you a million dollars to hear the solution to the problem (or a goal that would solve the problem)- what would you tell them?
   - What have you already tried to solve this problem? Tell me about the success of this.
   - How could we turn the solution to the problem into a SMART goal?

4. **Celebrate Successes**
   - How will you know once you've achieved your goal (aka- solved the problem)?
   - Now tell me about a time in the last month when you didn't have the problem. What was different about that time?
   - Tell me about a time since our last session when you were successful with your goal.
   - What were you doing when you were successful with your goal?

5. **Reflecting on Counseling Experience**
   - How did you/your parents/teachers/friends feel when you achieved your goal?
   - Tell me about how someone treated you differently once you started achieving your goal?
   - How did you react to this person treating you differently?
   - What are some other goals you might like to achieve?

# SESSION 2 Creating the SMART Goal

## TOPIC OVERVIEW

**The student will:**

- Continue building relationship with counselor
- Identify their self-chosen SMART goal
- Apply the components of the SMART goal to their own self-chosen goal
- Celebrate times when the problem didn't exist
- Generate specific behaviors to foster goal achievement

**Materials**

- New Reproducibles (attached at the end of this session):
  > Individual Counseling Notes Form
  > SMART Goal Information
  > SMART Goal Steps & Prompt
- Former Reproducibles:
  > Interest Form (completed from session 1)
  > The "3 Hurts" Emergency- should be prominently displayed where student can see it
  > My Scales (completed from session 1)
  > SFBC Questioning Guide (from session 1)
- Pencil
- Note cards

**Procedures**

1. **Welcome**
   - Welcome the student to the session and ask them to scale their week from 1-10 (1- worst to 10- best); have them explain why they have rated their week with this number.

   - If needed to break the ice, have the student share a few more of their Interest Form responses with you or ask them a few open-ended questions about their responses.

2. **Goal Work**
   - Review the problem that the student wanted to work on from the last session (if necessary, you can refer to the lowest numbered topic on the My Scales sheet from last session).

   - Ask the student to report on last session's homework to discuss if they had any more ideas on developing their goal.

   - Discuss how to turn their tentative goal into a SMART goal by explaining what a SMART goal is and applying each of the SMART characteristics to it. Write the student's SMART goal in the appropriate section "Student's SMART Goal" of the attached Individual Counseling Notes Form and on a note card for the student to take with them. See the SMART Goal Prompt reproducible at the end of this session for further explanation and a template.

   - If necessary, you can discuss some of the Step 3 questions from the SFBC Questioning sheet with the student in order to develop their goal further.

# SMART Goal Information

*Counselor Instructions & Information*

A SMART goal is a statement that specifically expresses what someone wants to achieve in a reasonable amount of time. This type of goal is an effective way to help students stay on track with what they are trying to achieve. Research shows that trauma often interferes with memory, making it even harder for some students to remember to consistently work towards their goal (NICAMB, 2017). For that reason, it is important to discuss and write down the SMART goal in every session so it stays fresh in the student's mind. Prepare a goal note with the student in session and then send it home with the student after the session as a reminder. Here are the components of a SMART goal, as well as steps and a template, so that you can guide your students in creating an effective goal for themselves.

*SMART Goals Posterette:*

## SMART goals are:

**S** — **SPECIFIC**
(Exactly what do you want to achieve?)

**M** — **MEASURABLE**
(What is the proof that you will see when you achieve your goal?)

**A** — **ACHIEVABLE**
(Can you realistically achieve your goal?)

**R** — **RELEVANT**
(Is your goal worthwhile for you to achieve?)

**T** — **TIME BOUND**
(When will you achieve your goal?)

# SMART Goal Steps & Prompt

*Counselor Instructions & Information*

**STEPS:**

1. Have the student write their goal during the session by copying and filling in the prompt below on a note card.
2. Also write the goal in the appropriate place on the Individual Counseling Notes Form.
3. Give student the goal note card as a reminder when they leave the session.
4. The next day, send a reminder note to cheer them on; you can even do this weekly for the rest of the semester. Below are some ideas for what to put on the reminder note:
   - A positive comment about something they did/discussed in the session.
   - A reminder of the specific behaviors to achieve their goal.
   - The session homework assignment.

*SMART Goal Template:*

**SMART Goal**

**By** ______________________, ______________________________

*(date goal will be achieved)* *(student name)*

**will** ____________________________________________;

*(specific, achievable goal)*

**we will know the goal has been achieved when** ______________

____________________________________________.

*(measurable data piece)*

**EXAMPLE SMART GOALS**

- By next week, Stephanie will keep her body to herself (not hit anyone); we will know the goal has been achieved when she has no discipline referrals for the week.
- By the next report card, Stephane will earn a 75% or better in math; we will know the goal has been achieved when we see a math A. B, or C on the report card.

SESSION 3

# Specific Behaviors & The Positive Change Cycle

## TOPIC OVERVIEW

**The student will:**

- Identify specific behaviors to foster goal achievement
- Explore the positive change cycle of behavior
- Share and celebrate goal successes

**Materials**

- New Reproducibles (attached at the end of this session):
  > Role Play
  > Feedback Form
  > How Am I Doing?
- Former Reproducibles:
  > Individual Counseling Notes Form
  > The "3 Hurts" Emergency- should be prominently displayed where student can see it
- Pencil
- Note cards

**Procedures**

1. **Welcome**
   - Welcome the student to the session and ask them to scale their week from 1-10 (1- worst to 10- best).
   - Have them explain why they have rated their week with this number.

2. **Goal Work**
   - Have the student use their goal note card to reference throughout the session; if they have misplaced it, have them recopy their goal from your Individual Counseling Notes Form (last session) onto a new note card.
   - Ask the student to read their goal aloud to review it.
   - If necessary, have the student also review the problem by taking a look back at their completed My Scales sheet from session 1.

3. **Success Sharing**
   - Ask the student to report on last session's homework to observe the times that they were successful with their goal.
   - Use the Million Dollar Question from the SFBC Questioning sheet (session 1 reproducible) if the student needs help identifying a success.
   - Praise the student for all goal successes–big and small!
   - If not discussed in the previous section, have the student tell you specific behaviors that they used this past week to achieve their goal; ask them for an update on how well the behaviors did or did not work. Refer back to Individual Counseling Notes Sheet from last session for these behaviors, if necessary.
   - Ask the student if additional specific behaviors are needed to achieve their goal- if so, add them to the student's note card. As needed, also notate them on this session's "The SMART goal will be achieved through these behaviors" section of the Individual Counseling Notes Form.

- In case you feel the student needs additional behaviors to achieve their goal, utilize the student's answers to Step 3 of SFBC Questioning sheet from session 1.

- Spend a few minutes role playing some of these specific behaviors with the student. Use the attached Role Play sheet for guidance on this activity.

4. **Positive Change Cycles**
   - Pose the following open-ended question: "How do the people in your life (friends, teachers, family members, etc.) treat you differently since you have started working on your goal and made these behavioral changes?"

   - Discuss the cyclical nature of positive change: when we change our behavior in a positive way, it influences the people around us to do the same. For example- if a student stops jumping out of his seat in class, the teacher will not reprimand the student for this anymore, the student then feels better about their school behavior and starts liking school more.

   - Tell the student that their Counseling Homework for this session is to continue observing the times that they are successful with their goal and also to notice when others treat them differently now that they have a goal.

5. **Feedback**
   - Explain to the student that it is important to get feedback from others on our goal because it helps us to know how we are progressing. Also, briefly discuss with them that positive relationships with others are one of the strongest ways to change ourselves and feel better, especially if something bad has happened to us. (Perry, 2017). Tell the student that this feedback will help improve and build relationships as well as learn more about goal achievement.

   - Read over the attached Feedback Form with the student and have them select a few adults that should complete the form.

**After the session, deliver these forms to the adults selected by the student. Before the next counseling session, collect the completed forms and summarize the adult comments on the form called "How Am I Doing?" Any negative comments that are not worded constructively should be omitted or re-worded. Make an extra copy of this completed form so that the student can take it home and share it with their family.*

6. **Wrap Up**
   - Praise the student for doing such challenging work in this session. Let the student know that you will continue working together on their goal in the next session. Discuss that the next session is the last scheduled session; advise the student about how they can request a follow up session and see you on an as-needed basis.

   - Ask the student if there is anything more they would like to discuss or need help with for this week.

   - Prep and send the student their reminder note on the following day.

# Role Play

## *Counselor Instructions & Information*

Dr. Karyn Purvis, the creator of the Trust-Based Relational Intervention (TBRI) trauma approach, characterizes role playing as a proactive strategy and preventive teaching measure, saying "it allows the child to practice appropriate responses to frustrations he or she many encounter" (Purvis et al, 2013, p. 18). In addition, role-playing is a key activity to help any student achieve their goal, whether they've experienced trauma or not. It allows the student to practice their goal-related specific behaviors in a safe environment. Therefore, it is crucial to devote a few minutes of every session to role playing some of their specific behaviors with the student. Use the following steps to facilitate role play:

**STEPS:**

1. Have the student select one of the specific behaviors on their goal note card to role play.

2. With the counselor acting as the instigator creating the problem situation for the student, allow the student to act out the specific behavior that they are trying to implement in order to achieve their goal. For example, if the specific behavior is to keep hands to self, the counselor might gently poke the student, who then might move away or say "Please stop poking me," instead of poking back.

3. Process the role play with a few guiding questions such as:
    - How did you feel while role playing?
    - What was easiest and most difficult for you in this role play situation?
    - How do you think practicing this role play will help you in your life?

***Resistant Students***

Sometimes students are resistant to participating in role-play exercises. Here are some ways to get resistant students involved in role-playing:

- Try letting the student do a reverse role play where the student begins by role-playing and practices the "opposite" of the specific behavior, then processes it through a "behavioral re-do" conversation, and then practices the correct behavior (Purvis et al., 2013). An example from Dr. Purvis and her colleagues is as follows: "We would practice 'showing respect' through a playful script, but first start by showing 'NO respect,' giving the youth an opportunity to play-act her aggression and her typically mouthy responses. Then we would follow with a behavioral re-do, and do the same skit with the young woman then practicing respectful words" (2013, p. 18).

- Try giving resistant students a pre-written role-playing skit that highlights their specific behavior so they can read aloud and follow their lines. This allows them to focus on practicing their behavior without the distraction of having to think through and act out an improvisation (Lerner, 2018).

- Spend 5 minutes of the session discussing what is causing their reluctance. Then spend an additional 5 minutes to guide them to the idea that practicing their specific behaviors in a safe environment is necessary in order to achieve their goal that they chose for themselves. During this discussion, it is helpful to address how practice situations may feel silly but give us the skills we need to calm ourselves when the stress or conflict is overwhelming. Give them the analogy of a professional athlete's practice leading up to game day: every professional athlete must spend hours practicing against his/her own teammates to prepare for that one- or two-hour game against the competing athlete(s) on game day.

# Feedback Form

*Staff Reproducible*

**As you may know, I have been working with student, ________________________________________,**

**on his/her goal of ________________________________________________________________.**

**We would really like your thoughts on how he/she is doing outside of our counseling sessions. Please answer the following questions and I will collect this completed form from you on the date: ____________________.**

**Thank you so much.**

**Sincerely,**

______________________________________________

*Counselor*

1. Please list all successes (both big and small) you have observed related to the student achieving the goal.

_______________________________________________________________

_______________________________________________________________

2. Please write any additional actions that you feel the student must do to achieve their goal.

_______________________________________________________________

_______________________________________________________________

3. Are there any other behaviors that you feel the student should work on to achieve their goal?

_______________________________________________________________

_______________________________________________________________

# How Am I Doing?

*Student Reproducible*

*Directions: Your counselor has written your teacher feedback on this form for you to review. Read over and discuss your "Glows" and "Grows" with your counselor. Take this form home and share it with your family, too.*

## GLOWS

## GROWS

# SESSION 4 Celebrations!

**TOPIC OVERVIEW**

**The student will:**

- Review their goal and the behaviors they need to achieve goal
- Celebrate their goal and behavior successes
- Reflect on and evaluate their overall counseling experience

**Materials**

- New Reproducibles (attached at the end of this session):
  > My Scales (new copy will serve as counseling posttest, make a fresh copy of the session 1 reproducible)
  > Completed How Am I Doing? form with additional copy for student
  > Student Evaluation
- Former Reproducibles:
  > Individual Counseling Notes Form
  > The "3 Hurts" Emergency- should be prominently displayed where student can see it
  > My Scales (completed original copy from session 1)
- Pencil
- Note cards

**Procedures**

1. **Welcome**
   - Welcome the student to the session and ask them to scale their week from 1-10 (1- worst to 10- best).
   - Have them explain why they have rated their week with this number.
   - Remind the student that this is their final scheduled session with you; ask if they want a follow-up session, and if so, schedule it. The follow-up session activities are listed in the recommendations section of this guide.
2. **Goal/Behaviors Review & Success Sharing**
   - Have the student use their goal note card to reference throughout the session; if they have misplaced it, have them recopy their goal from your Individual Counseling Notes Form (last session) onto a new note card.
   - Ask the student to read their goal/specific behaviors aloud to review.
   - Ask the student to report on last session's homework of observing:
     > the times that they were successful with their goal (and/or any specific behaviors related to it).
     > when/how others treat them differently now that they have a goal.
   - Use the Million Dollar Question from the SFBC Questioning Sheet (session 1 reproducible) if the student needs help identifying a success.
   - Praise the student for all goal successes.
   - Spend a few minutes role playing some of these specific behaviors with the student.

SESSION 4

# Celebrations!

**Procedures** *(continued)*

3. **Feedback**
   - Go over the responses on the How Am I Doing? form with the student; be sure to start with the positives ("Glows") first.
   - Gently discuss the "Grows" also by applying them to the student's goal and specific behaviors. Give the student a copy of this form to take home and share with their family.

4. **Evaluation**
   - Complete a new My Scales form with student. Together, compare their session 1 and session 4 My Scales sheets, in order to identify changes and progress. Collect and keep both My Scales sheets to use for data purposes.
   - Complete the attached Student Evaluation by reading each statement to the student and then having them write their response. Alternately the student can dictate their responses to you. Collect and keep for data purposes.

5. **Wrap Up**
   - Praise the student for doing such challenging work to achieve their goal.
   - Question the student if there is anything more they would like to discuss.
   - Remind the student of how to access you for future sessions, as needed.

# Student Evaluation

*Student Reproducible*

*Congratulations on completing this goal work program! Making changes in your life and setting goals for yourself is hard work, but the success you experience as a result of accomplishing goals feels awesome. Please take a few minutes now to reflect on what you've learned and then answer the following questions.*

1. What have you learned about yourself through our sessions?

___

___

2. How will these learnings affect you in the future?

___

___

3. Would you recommend these sessions to a friend? Why or Why not?

___

___

4. Which activities did you find most and least useful?

___

___

5. Additional Comments:

___

___

# Additional Activities

## *Counselor Instructions & Information*

As mentioned in the recommendations section, these are additional activities for extending your sessions. These activities have been created to extend the counseling experience past the four sessions that are typically provided in a school counseling setting. I've included some tips below on how to use these additional activities to create sessions 5-8. In addition, these activities can be added into existing sessions if you'd like to extend the length of your individual sessions past 1 hour. You can also substitute any of the additional activities for a particular session activity if that activity won't work with your student.

**TIPS FOR SESSIONS 5-8**

- Continue to follow the same basic structure of the sessions provided in this Way to Goal guide, while adding in the additional activity. Here are the procedures for sessions 4 through 7.
  > Welcome
  > Goal/Behavior Review
  > Homework Shareout
  > Celebrate Successes
  > Additional Activity (listed below)
  > Wrap Up

- Move this guide's session 4 evaluation activities (student evaluation, end-of-counseling scaling, etc.) to session 8 in the above "additional activity" bullet.

- Keep in mind that individual counseling provided by the school counselor in the school setting should be short-term (approximately four sessions), according to the American School Counselor Association (ASCA, 2016).

**STAIRWAY BREATHING**

This activity is great for helping students to focus on their goal and to regain a sense of control. Oftentimes, at the start of goal work, the student feels overwhelmed by all that is "wrong" in their life; they can become even further overwhelmed when the issues that need to be "fixed" are out of their control (as is often the case for children living in dysfunctional families). Teach the student this breathing exercise to empower them and show them that they do have control over a goal they want to achieve. Follow these steps to lead the student through Stairway Breathing:

1. Explain to the student that they will learn a breathing exercise to help them feel better and achieve their goal. Tell them that in the exercise, they will imagine going down a flight of stairs, taking one step down every time they exhale. At the bottom of the stairs is a door to a room where they will feel safe, free of distraction, and able to focus on their goal.

2. With eyes closed, lead the student through the exercise by breathing with them as you narrate yourself exhaling as you descend each step. After about 5-10 steps, arrive at the door, again narrating how you are opening it and entering a room that is safe and distraction-free. With the student, take 3-5 deep breaths in the room, explaining how the distractions slip away as you take control of your goal.

3. Process the activity with the student by asking them how they feel, what they liked/disliked about activity, and what thoughts they are having about their goal.

### THE RELAXER

This technique uses a simple hand-face meditative movement to activate the parasympathetic system. Dr. Nadine Burke, the surgeon general of California and an advocate for traumatized children explains, "meditation activates the resting-and-digesting system (also called the parasympathetic nervous system). The parasympathetic nervous system is responsible for things like lowering heart rate and blood pressure, and it directly counters the effects of the stress response. Given the profound connection between the stress response and the neurological, hormonal, and immune systems, a calmer, healthier mind seemed like a good place to start reversing the effects of toxic stress [trauma]." (Burke, 2018, p. 112). We can actually touch a parasympathetic point on our body in order to calm ourselves down during times of stress or upset! One of these points is the area between the nose and upper lip, so holding your index finger on it or running your finger across it can produce a feeling of relaxation. Explain this to the student and lead them through an exercise where they place their index finger under their nose, curving around and touching their upper lip. While they hold their finger in this position, have them take 5 deep breaths- in through their nose and out through their mouth. Process the exercise by asking them how they felt during it and how they might use it while feeling stressed at school or at home.

### SALT IN HIS SHOES

*Salt in his Shoes* tells the story of how a young Michael Jordan turned his failures into successes, as told by his mother. He had a goal of playing basketball, and despite being short and not very good at it, he went for it! The topic and incredible illustrations of this book make it very engaging for elementary students all the way up to high schoolers! Read this book with your student and process the book's themes of goal achievement and growth mindset by discussing the following questions:

Discussion Questions:

- Tell about some life challenges that Michael experiences.
- How do his challenges affect his basketball game negatively?
- What is MJ's goal? How does he go about achieving it?
- What is your goal? What similarities and differences do you notice in how both you and MJ are achieving your goals?
- What does Michael's Dad tell him and why?
- How does Michael's talk with his dad cause success?
- What did you learn about overcoming challenges from the story?

### MAKING A CHANGE IN YOUR LIFE

Kidshealth.org is a fantastic website (with a teen section, as well) with many different goal achievement resources that you can use with your student in a session. My favorite one is called "Making a Change in Your Life" and it is featured on the Teenshealth side of the site (though this activity is very appropriate for upper elementary students as well as middle and high schoolers). To facilitate this activity with your student, follow these steps:

1. Go to https://kidshealth.org/en/teens/make-change.html?WT.ac=ctg or type "Making a Change in Your Life" into the Kidshealth.org search bar.

2. Read the text on the page together and then click "Get Started" in the Your Personal Plan box.

3. Work through the prompts with the student, applying their note card goal and/or specific behaviors to the tasks in the activity.

Alternately, you might just head over to the site and search the key word "goals" to see all the options you can use in an individual session.

# Data Analysis

## *Counselor Instructions & Information*

Data is crucial to show the importance and relevance of any counseling intervention. Collecting and compiling data is never easy and takes time, but no counseling program is complete without it! Below is a comprehensive way to show your individual data, along with some tips and explanations on how to compile the data. It takes a few hours to compile the six data parts, and you can use as many or as few of the parts below in your data reports. It is best to wait about 1 month after the individual sessions have ended before compiling the data in order to get the most complete and up-to-date information.

**PART ONE: TITLE, DATE, AND DESCRIPTION**

**Explanation: In this part, include the title of the counseling sessions, the semester and year they occurred, and a brief description of the topics covered.**

**SAMPLE**

Way to Goal, Fall Semester 20___

*Way to Goal* is an individual psychoeducational counseling program for children who are struggling with a challenging life situation or who just want to achieve success in a certain area of their life such as school. Each session consists of activities that guide the process of goal achievement using solution focused brief counseling techniques.

**PART TWO: STUDENT EVALUATION**

**Explanation: In this part, include a brief summary of the student evaluation instrument (see Student Evaluation from session 4) and some meaningful quotes from the evaluation, showing what the child learned during the experience.**

**SAMPLE**

The student completes a short evaluation during the final session to evaluate the individual counseling experience–what went well, what didn't go well, how the sessions have helped them, what they still need help with, etc.

*As a result of this counseling experience, I learned...*

- *that my family problems don't have to stop my goals.*
- *how to set a goal for myself.*
- *that I can achieve any goal I set my mind to!*
- *how to deal with problems.*

**PART THREE: SCALING (PRE/POSTTEST) RESULTS**

**Explanation: In this part, compile the student's scaling numbers from the first and last session into the chart below, using an Excel spreadsheet. Then highlight the chart in Excel and click on Insert tab in the ribbon of commands, next click on the first tiny graph icon ("Insert Column Chart") and choose the first 2D Column; this automatically turns the chart into a graph. Once the chart has been created, you can customize it using one of the design options Excel offers; keep it clear as well as easy on yourself by using layout 9 in the "Chart Layouts" area of the Chart Tools ribbon.**

**SAMPLE CHART & BAR GRAPH**

| | SCHOOL | HOME | ME |
|---|---|---|---|
| Pretest Scaling–first session | 5 | 1 | 7 |
| Posttest Scaling–last session | 6 | 4 | 10 |

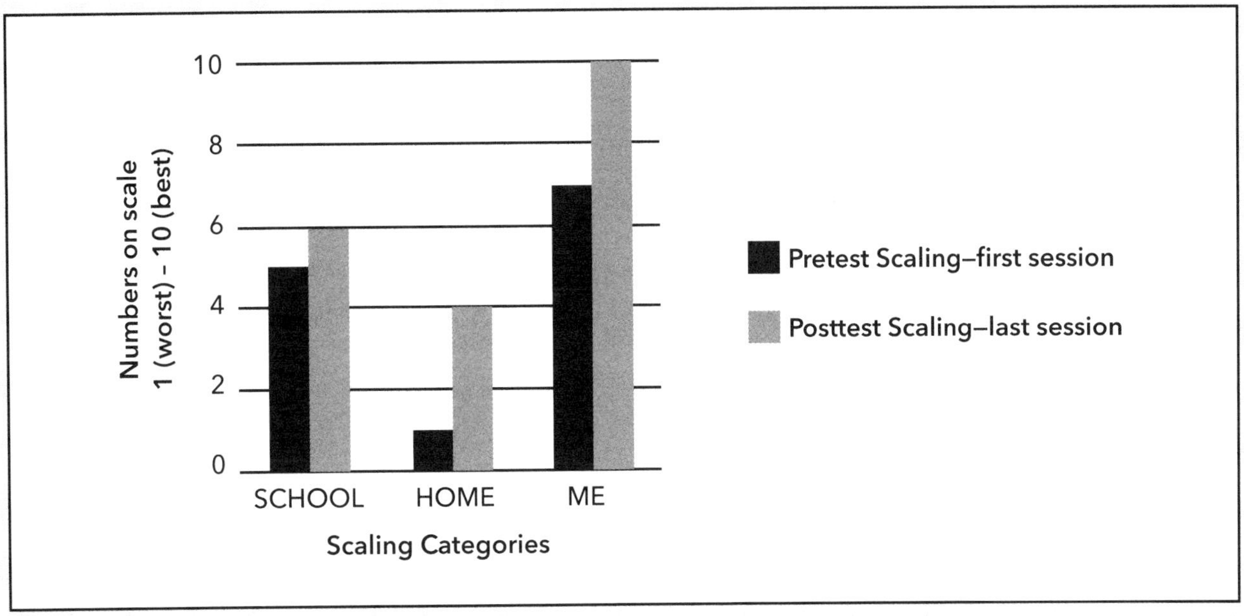


**PART FOUR: GRADE AVERAGES**

Explanation: In this part, analyze the grades of the student for the term before, the term during, and the term after the individual sessions. Plug the number of passing grades the student achieved before, during, and after the counseling experience into the first chart below. Then, use the data in the first chart to calculate the increases in the number of classes they passed in the second chart. This shows how the individual counseling experience has contributed to improved student academic achievement. See sample below.

**SAMPLE CHART & BAR GRAPH**

| | Number of Passing Classes in Term BEFORE Counseling Sessions | Number of Passing Classes in Term DURING Counseling Sessions | Number of Passing Classes in Term AFTER Counseling Sessions |
|---|---|---|---|
| Student X | 5 | 7 | 4 |

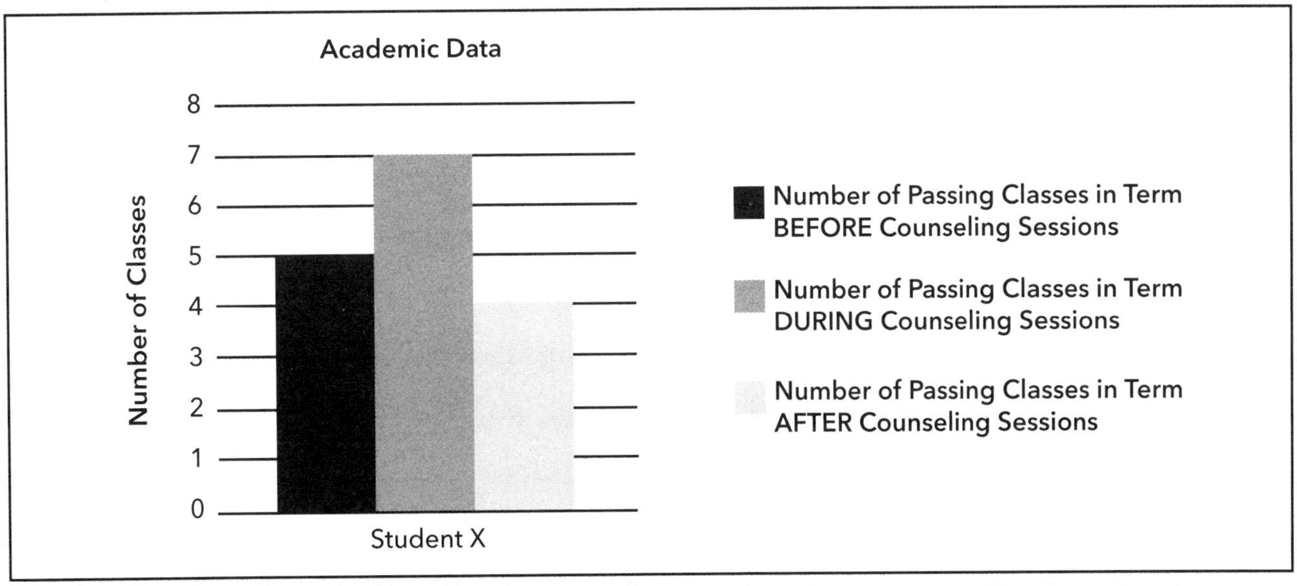

**PART FIVE: DISCIPLINARY REFERRALS**

**Explanation: In this part, analyze the discipline referrals of the student in the term before, the term during and the term after the counseling sessions. Plug all discipline referrals received in the terms before, during, and after the sessions into the first chart below and then use the data in the first chart to calculate decreases in discipline referrals in the second chart. This shows how the individual counseling experience has contributed to improved student behavior. See sample below.**

**SAMPLE CHART & BAR GRAPH**

| | Number of Disciplinary Referrals in Term BEFORE Counseling Sessions | Number of Disciplinary Referrals in Term DURING Counseling Sessions | Number of Disciplinary Referrals in Term AFTER Counseling Sessions |
|---|---|---|---|
| Student X | 5 | 1 | 0 |

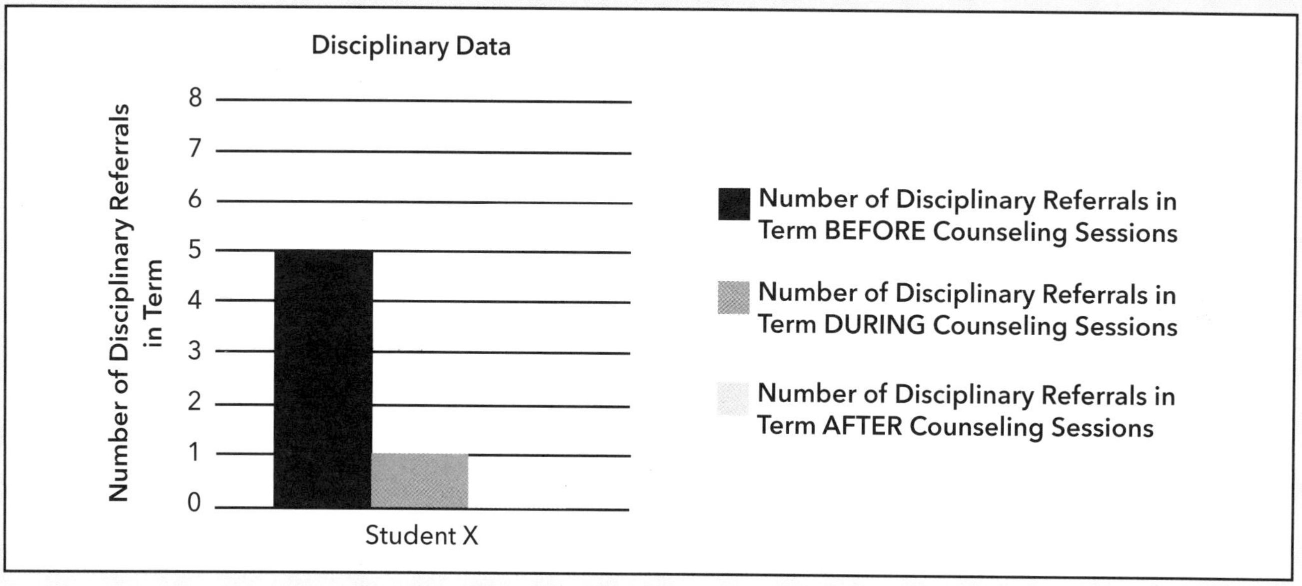


**PART SIX: SUMMARY OF DATA**

**Explanation: In this part, analyze all the charts and graphs in parts 3–5 and write a summary that explains the data trends for campus stakeholders.**

**SAMPLE**

The scaling pre/posttest chart and bar graph shows that the student rated himself as feeling significantly better after the individual counseling experience. The student found that as he started to feel better about himself and learn that he could achieve his own goals despite his family circumstances, his school performance started to improve. The student requested to start goal-based group counseling next semester in order to continue working on his grades goal! His home number also increased, though the student remarked that because he doesn't have the power to change his parents' life choices (resulting in the family's past traumatic experiences), he doesn't expect that number to ever rise much higher than a five.

During the academic term in which the counseling sessions occurred, the student was able to increase his number of passing classes to seven out of eight total classes! The fact that the student's number of passing classes declined from seven to only four passing classes after individual counseling concluded indicates the need to explore whether further counseling is needed.

The student had five disciplinary referrals before the counseling sessions, which decreased to just one referral during counseling and zero referrals after counseling ended!

***Troubled children are in some kind of pain—and pain makes people irritable, anxious, and aggressive.***

Dr. Bruce Perry, *The Boy Who Was Raised as A Dog*

## A "Hard Places" Group Story

I have experienced this quote firsthand in running counseling groups that included children who had experienced trauma, as I'm sure many of you have also. Often these negative emotions would spread to the non-trauma members, due to the brain's tendency to take on the habits, emotions, and attitudes of those around us. I remember one group in particular where irritability and apathy was on display in almost every session. No matter what activities I brought to the table, the group members usually responded with sighs and eye rolls. It was a healthy coping skills group, made up of mostly teen girls who had experienced various traumatic incidents in their young lives. Though they came to group dutifully each week and were very attentive to all group activities, they just didn't seem to enjoy it… until one day when I brought a silly, babyish picture book to group. We were several sessions in and I had been to a counselor convention the week before and had purchased, ***How Are You Feeling, Juan Pablo Chameleon?*** by Dan St. Romain. I had fallen madly in love with this book—it is a sweet and delightful story that perfectly embodies various positive coping habits with bursts of vibrant color on every page. I figured the group would roll their eyes at it, but I was determined to use the book in group. Well, wouldn't you know, they loved this book. I mean, they LOVED it! They perked right up as soon as I showed it to them, there were no eye rolls at my obvious enthusiasm over the book, and they silently took in every page with wide eyes as I read it to them. I asked them why this book got such a positive reaction from them when they appeared uninterested in the other group activities, but their response to this was just more eye rolling, sighs, and protests of, "Miss, we LIKE the group activities. Gosh!" No one could give me a definitive answer over why this book sparked such a difference in their affect.

As I reflected on that surprising group session over the next week, I turned back to Dr. Perry for my answer. After discussing the irritability of troubled kids, he goes on to say, "Only patient, loving, consistent care works; there are no short-term miracle cures." (2014, p. 274). And that's what I hadn't realized- these students needed patience and time to heal in group, which is why they kept coming back, session after session, even though they seemed unexcited. Moreover, when I brought in that charming little picture book, it met them right where they were emotionally and, to use the words of Dr. Perry, with loving care! Most of these group members had never gotten to experience sweet, babyish picture books during the harsh experiences of their formative years, so when I brought one into group, they took to the love and sweetness in the book like bees to a flower. Later, when we did our final group experience evaluations, every single one of them stated that the book experience was their favorite group activity.

So, what does this mean for running your own best practice, trauma-informed group? Well, it simply means that best practice IS trauma-informed. Keep in mind that not every student in my group described above had experienced trauma, but all of them responded favorably to the patience and time that the group setting provided. Fortunately, these two characteristics are inherent in the nature of group counseling as students return, session after session, to learn psychoeducational skills in a kind, nurturing, and repetitive manner. And the picture book I shared exposed my hardened teen group members to a little burst of loving kindness in the form of a sweet story with charming illustrations. My group also loved the Juan Pablo Chameleon book because it met them where they were developmentally by giving them information about positive coping habits through bright pictures with cute animal faces.

So, what are the key characteristics of the trauma-informed group? In the school setting, they are usually psychoeducational which means they help members to gain information and develop skills for challenging situations through education-based techniques (Corey et al., 2017). Each session should include various trauma-informed group counseling strategies such as goal work and positive coping habits. Discussing, setting, and achieving goals is a key to building grit and resilience which are important protective factors against trauma. Moreover, the solution focused brief counseling (SFBC) techniques of unconditional positive regard and perspective-changing are just as effective in the group setting as they are in the individual counseling setting that we covered in the previous section of this book. In addition, the strong relationships formed in the group setting help students make even more progress with the SFBC strategies of reaching goals and providing feedback (Murphy, 2008). Finally, warmth and neutrality are important characteristics in all effective counselors, but are especially important in the leader of a trauma-informed group. Additionally, it is crucial for the counselor to demonstrate firmness in their expectations that members adhere to the group norms. Keep in mind that students of trauma often need an extra safe and structured group setting, which is why warmth, neutrality, and firmness are so important (Hubbs, 2004).

So, in the spirit of facilitating best practice groups that will allow any struggling child to thrive, I propose the following recommendations.

## Recommendations for Facilitating Group Counseling

### *Starting the Counseling Group*

- This section of the book has a group counseling guide with 6 sessions of one hour each. Each session can be easily shortened by omitting some of the activities if you have less time for group sessions or are working with younger group members. Keep in mind that for some trauma-informed groups, less is more because students with anxiety or processing issues may have trouble keeping up with multiple steps- in this case, feel free to omit activities to simplify sessions. Alternately, the sessions can also be lengthened by adding in some additional activities provided at the end of this group counseling guide.

- After this group recommendations section, a lesson plan for each group session is provided with the accompanying reproducible worksheets and resources needed for that session. At the end of the group guide, additional activities and data templates are compiled for easy reference.

- This resource has various leveled topics/activities, making it appropriate for children in grades three through high school. It was developed for students in a school setting, but it can easily be modified for use in a clinical or even virtual setting. Each session has trauma-informed techniques that will support both students of trauma and students who have not been exposed to trauma. Here are some ways to use this guide with very young students:
  - Shorten or simplify some of the lists/cards in the sessions.
  - Have group members dictate writing activities rather than writing on their own.
  - Create a template that members can copy rather than writing on their own.

  > Substitute an Additional Activity (provided at the end of the counseling guide) for any session activities that seem too mature for elementary students.
  > The counselor/ reads session passages aloud while the group members follow along with their finger.

- This session guide can be easily adapted for the virtual school counseling setting by following all of the steps below on a FERPA-compliant online platform such as Zoom or Google Hangouts. If needed, here is a link to find various sets of directions on how to set up Google Hangouts so you can meet with the students in a virtual group: https://support.google.com/hangouts. Take some time to set it up and then practice using it with a family member or a colleague first, just so you have it down. Additionally, you can modify some of the partner and group work by having one pair practice at time or by assigning the group work as homework to be done with a family member. For example, the nature walk can be done alone off platform or with the whole family, then have the member share their nature walk experience and process the discussion questions in the next group session. Moreover, written work such as goal note cards, pre/posttests, and final evaluations can be done through an online comments/Q&A feature or simply by having members email their responses to you. Furthermore, encourage students to creatively find certain session materials in their own homes that they can use in group; for example, you can teach students how to make their own mandala by using the instructions in the session 5 activity. Finally, 30-35 minutes might be more than enough time for a group session in the virtual setting; as a result, feel free to remove any activities that don't flow as well in the virtual setting. The key in facilitating group work in the virtual setting is flexibility; with a bit of patience and tweaking, trauma-informed groups can run just as effectively in both types of settings.

- Alternately, older group members might act like they are too mature or "grown up" for counseling activities. For these situations, just keep in mind that the counselor sets the tone for the group session; therefore, if you are enthusiastic and comfortable with the activities, your older group members will come around. Likewise, if you feel awkward, juvenile, and self-conscious about certain activities, the students will mirror these feelings.

- Four to eight members is an ideal number of group participants, with some groups needing to stay closer to the four-member mark and other groups that can easily be expanded to eight (or even ten) members. Typically, groups with high-energy, irritable, or disruptive students should be kept small.

- It is best to meet once per week in a quiet, private room or area.

- This is a psychoeducational sessions guide. It should be used to educate students on wellness and school success. It should not be used as a substitute for mental health therapy with a licensed practitioner.

- Group counseling strategies generally create feelings of hopefulness, connectedness to others, and bonding. These feelings are crucial to helping students heal. As a result of these naturally occurring characteristics in the group setting, it is often a good fit for students experiencing trauma. Furthermore, traumatized students can grapple with feelings of isolation and social anxieties; luckily, the group counseling setting naturally provides support, connection, and social interaction which serve as protective factors against these struggles. Use the group setting to create opportunities for building hope and normalizing stress reactions. Guiding students to use their strengths in creating solutions for themselves is also an empowering protective factor (Hubbs, 2004). These protective factors are a key to building resilience and grit.

- This group guide can be used with almost any student who is able to follow the group rules and meets the following screening criteria. However, here are a few questions to consider when you have a student with a severe trauma or a student whose trauma is very different from the other group members' experiences:
  > Is the child able to relate to the other group members?
  > Is the trauma too recent or severe for the student to process at this time?
  > Is the child able to share his/her feelings?
  > Will the child feel safe being exposed to other members' experiences? (Hubbs, 2004).

- Additionally, students demonstrating the following issues are generally not best served through the psychoeducational school counseling group experience. It is better to refer them out to a licensed mental health provider.
  > psychosis
  > homicidal ideation
  > active suicidal ideation
  > inability to interact with other children
  > severe denial
  > active substance abuse (Hubbs, 2004).

- It is important to screen members for inclusion in the group before the group starts. You can begin this process with an informal needs assessment given to teachers and school staff. An example is provided following this explanation. You can also modify the example to use with students and parents/guardians. Have defined expectations for the students in group; these expectations should be based on data. Determine data-based group criteria that students referred for group counseling must meet in order to be enrolled in a group. For example, your group criteria might be "student is failing at least 2 classes" and/or "student has at least 3 discipline referrals", etc. Meet briefly with each prospective group member individually to discuss the group topic/purpose. If they are interested in participating in the group, give them the permission form (included with session 1) so they can take it home for their parent/ guardian to sign and return it to you.

    *Hello Staff,*
    ***The School Counseling Office will be starting counseling groups for struggling students next month. If you have students you would like to add to these groups, please email back the student's ID# and the group you'd like them to be in. We'd like this info by next Monday, so we can start the process of screening prospective group members and getting parental consent.***
    *Thank You,*
    *Your School Counselors*

- Keep a Group Binder with a separate section for each group you run. The binder should contain your Group Notes sheet, students' schedules/teachers, permission forms (included with session 1) and any handouts you will use.

- Plan each session using the Group Notes sheet included with session 1; you will need to make a copy of it for sessions 2 through 6).

- Each session ends with discussion questions. The questions are provided as additional opportunities to process or lengthen the session, as needed.

## *Leading the Counseling Group*

- In every session, demonstrate careful adherence to the Group Rules & Consequences (included in with session 1). The use of fair, simple, and consistent group rules/consequences is essential to the success of a trauma-informed group! "Because trauma causes an overload of the stress response systems, which is marked by a loss of control, treatment of traumatized children must start by creating an atmosphere of safety. This is done most easily and effectively in the context of a predictable, respectful relationship" (Perry, 2014, p. 170). Here are a few important tips about using group rules to create predictability and respect within the group.
    - Post a printout of the rules sheet in the group room. Explain each of the group rules to the members and make sure special attention is paid to group rule #2 about confidentiality. Remember that confidentiality among minors cannot be guaranteed and this needs to be addressed with the group members. For example, I might say that we can't force anyone to keep confidentiality, so it is important for group members to be careful about what they choose to share in group. It is also important to address the limits of confidentiality at this time, as well.
    - Correct any group member not following a rule by gently asking them to read it aloud to the group. For students of trauma, I am especially careful to use a non-threatening tone when I ask them to read the rule they didn't follow. It is crucial to follow the consequence of having a private meeting after the group session with any member who is repeatedly not following the group rules.
    - In the private meeting, discuss the rule/s being broken and come up with a solution for following it. Remind the student of the solution right before the subsequent group sessions and the problem should fix itself. If the student continues to break the group rule/s, consider referring them out to a therapist for individual counseling.

- Use the group members' responses to the Group Evaluation (included with session 1) each week to plan your next session. Details on how to lead students through this informal evaluation are provided at the end of each session plan.

- During the first few minutes of a session, as group members trickle in, ask if anyone wants to discuss anything on their mind or from the previous week. In school settings, this is also a good time to address any discipline problems related to the group topic that might have occurred with a group member in the last week. Try to keep these discussions to no more than 5–10 minutes so as to not focus the entire session on them; set a timer if necessary. Also, for group members that want to discuss a traumatic experience- gently remind the group that the focus of the session is on goal work and positive coping habits, then guide the members back to that theme. Tell the trauma-talking student that you would like to address their experience individually right after the group ends. Follow up on this by meeting with the student after group to determine if their traumatic experience warrants a referral to parent/guardian or an outside agency.

- During the beginning of each session, it is good to review the optional homework assignment if you gave one during the previous session. As noted by Sohby and Cavellaro (2010), a homework assignment "also offers [students] an opportunity to understand the link between their actions and consequences and how they could use this information to result in future desirable results (p. 5)". However, this homework is optional, so you can skip it if the group session runs long and there is no time.

- There are some sharing and reading opportunities in these sessions. Always make sure to remind group members that they can say "pass" anytime they do not want to read aloud or share.

## *Ending the Counseling Group*

- Collecting group data helps to improve future groups and promote the counseling program with school stakeholders such as parents, administrators, and staff. Included after session six is an extensive six-part data plan that allows you to present all aspects of your group's successes to counseling program stakeholders.

- A follow-up session is an important SFBC technique that supports students even after their group has ended. It requires a well-organized process in much the same way that your sessions are run (Sklare, 2014). The main point of having a follow-up session after the group terminates is to check in on group members' experiences and to provide another opportunity for empowering them by celebrating their successes. Here are the steps for a follow-up session:
  - Take attendance on the group notes sheet and review the group rules (both included with session 1).
  - Ask group members if there is anything they want to discuss.
  - Hand out the photocopied goals and have each member read their goal aloud and share a success they have had with their goal recently.
  - Review the Positive Coping Habits reproducible from session 2 and then lead them through each group member's favorite PCH from the list. If the favorite doesn't lend itself to group practice, instead have the group member explain why it is their favorite.

- I have included suggestions for additional activities (included after session 6) if you'd like to extend the length of your group sessions past 1 hour or if you'd like to have more than six sessions. You can also substitute any of the additional activities for a particular session activity if that activity won't work with your group member population.

- If you would like to learn more about any of the strategies or activities in this book, please refer to the professional sources listed in the references at the end of this book.

# American School Counselor Association
# STANDARDS ALIGNMENT

The American School Counselor Association (ASCA) sets the national framework for a model school counseling program. As a result, The Support Cohort session activities are aligned with the following ASCA Mindsets & Behaviors that can be applied to the domains of Academic Development and Personal/Social Development.

**MINDSETS**

| | |
|---|---|
| M 1. | Belief in development of whole self, including a healthy balance of mental, social/emotional and physical well-being |
| M 2. | Self confidence in the ability to succeed |

**BEHAVIORS**

| | |
|---|---|
| B-SMS 1. | Demonstrate ability to assume responsibility |
| B-SS 2. | Create positive and supportive relationships with other students |
| B-SMS 5. | Demonstrate perseverance to achieve long- and short-term goals |
| B-SMS 7. | Demonstrate effective coping skills when faced with a problem |
| B-SMS 10. | Demonstrate ability to manage transitions and ability to adapt to changing situations and responsibilities |

(ASCA, 2019, p.3)

GROUP SESSION 1

# Getting to Know You

## TOPIC OVERVIEW

**The group member will:**

- Start building rapport with other group members
- Identify the purpose of the group
- Discuss group rules
- Identify the components of a SMART goal
- Make a SMART goal for success in school
- Explore the grounding technique as a positive coping practice

**Materials**

- Reproducibles: Group Notes, Coloring Mandala, Scaling Thermometer, Pre/Posttest, Growing with Grounding, SMART Goal Posterette and the SMART Goal Template (both from the Way to Goal guide, pages 22 & 23), Parent Permission Letter, Group Notes Sheet, Group Evaluation, and Group Rules & Consequences

- Items: note cards, crayons or markers, pencils, a healthy snack and some water for the grounding activity (if possible)

**Procedures**

**Sometimes this initial session can run a bit long, taking more than an hour. If necessary, you can save the grounding and the scaling activities for session 2.*

1. As students arrive, take attendance on the Group Notes sheet and offer students a coloring mandala to color as they wait for the session to begin.

2. Ask group members to explain the purpose of the group. Guide them towards the idea that they will support each other to healthfully handle adversity, feel better, and increase their school success.

3. Display the rules poster and briefly discuss they meaning of each rule.

4. Give each group member a Scaling Thermometer sheet. Discuss what scaling is with the group. Next, model how to color the thermometer to show where you are on its scale regarding how your day is going. Then have each student color to their scale number and explain to the group why they have chosen this number. Also use this sharing time for students to introduce themselves to the group with name, grade, and a success or goal they have achieved in their life.

5. Hand out the pretest and read the pretest statements aloud as group members mark Yes or No/I Don't Know for each statement. Collect and save these pretests until the last group session. **If your group members are very young or struggle with writing, consider reducing the pre/posttest items to 3.*

6. Introduce students to grounding as a relaxation technique that they can use to feel better if they are having a bad day. Use the Growing with Grounding reproducible to lead students through this exercise.

7. Display the SMART Goal Posterette. Tell group members that they will now create a SMART goal for themselves. Briefly explain what a SMART goal is by pointing out what each of the capital letters stands for on the SMART Goal Posterette.

# Getting to Know You

**Procedures** *(continued)*

8. Have group members think about one thing that is not going well for them at school and how they would like to improve it. Be sure to model this first so members can observe how you identify what is not going well at school and then how you will improve it. Show members the SMART Goal Template and demonstrate how to copy it on a note card.

9. Next, have each group member write their SMART goal on the note card. They should also read their goal aloud to the group while the group checks each goal to make sure it is SMART. To do this, after a member reads their goal, you can read each SMART goal component off the SMART Goal Posterette while the group members give a thumbs up if the goal incorporates that component or a thumbs down if it does not incorporate the component. Choose a proficient group member to help the struggling member change their goal, if necessary. **If your group members are very young or struggle with writing, consider having them draw their goal or give them a pre-printed note card with a simplified version of the SMART Goal Template already on it so all they have to do is copy their specific goal behavior into the prompt (or you can have them dictate the goal to you to fill in).*

10. Collect the goal note cards. Photocopy the note cards after group and give group members a copy the following day as a reminder to work toward their SMART goal during the week. Keep the originals for the next group session.

11. Display the group evaluation from your Group Notes sheet by enlarging it for all members to see. Complete the group evaluation by reading each evaluation statement aloud while the group members hold up the corresponding number of fingers to indicate their responses. Tally the group members' responses on the Group Notes sheet to use in future session planning.

**Optional Homework Activity**

- Share your SMART goal with a family member. Ask your family member to tell you about an experience they have had with a goal they want/ed to achieve.

**Discussion Questions**

- What are you most curious about learning in this group experience? Explain.
- How did you feel when you solved a problem in your life? Tell us about this experience and explain your feelings.
- What was the reason you chose the SMART goal you wrote on your card?

# Parent/Guardian Permission Letter

Date: ____________________

Dear Parent/Guardian:

The Counseling Program at ________________________________ School includes group counseling sessions. Your child ______________________________, has been referred for participation in short-term group counseling. With your permission, your child will attend six sessions on a scheduled basis at school by the counselor. These sessions will focus on the topic of ___________________________________________________________. The sessions will not change the child's academic program. Participation in the sessions is voluntary, and confidentiality will be discussed and respected.

At times, the counselor and school-based staff (principal, assistant principal, social worker, psychologist, behavior specialist, teacher, nurse, etc.) will need to exchange information about your child (goals, strategies, etc.). All communication will take place only on an educational need-to-know basis.

This permission is for the school year______.

If you would like for your child to have group counseling sessions with the counselor, please sign and return this form to the counseling office. If you have any questions or concerns, please call ________________________.

Thank you,

________________________________________________________

Counselor

I give permission for ____________________________________ to participate in group counseling sessions.

________________________________________________

Parent/Guardian Signature

________________________________________________

Phone Number

## Group Notes

*Counselor Information Sheet*

Group Name ______________________ **SESSION #** ___ Date ______________

> Activities:

______________________________________________

______________________________________________

______________________________________________

> Summary of Session:

______________________________________________

______________________________________________

______________________________________________

| Group Member | Attended? | Questions & Points to Work on/Discuss | Teacher Comments |
|---|---|---|---|
| | | | |
| | | | |
| | | | |
| | | | |
| | | | |
| | | | |

> Session Critique by Group Members:

| Behaviors | Agree - 3 | Sort of - 2 | Disagree - 1 |
|---|---|---|---|
| The group members listened to me. | | | |
| What we did/discussed was important/helpful to me. | | | |
| I hope we do the same kind of things next time. | | | |

# Coloring Mandala

*Student Reproducible*

*Directions: Please color in the mandala below as you wait for group to start.*

# Scaling Thermometer

*Student Reproducible*

*Scaling is a way to use numbers to show how we are feeling and how our day or week is going. Think about how your day is going and how you are feeling. Decide on a number 1-10 (with 10 as the best) to show this. Color your thermometer up to this number. Be ready to introduce yourself to the group with your name, grade, and what success or goal you have achieved in your life so far. Then show the group your thermometer and explain why you have chosen your particular scaling number.*

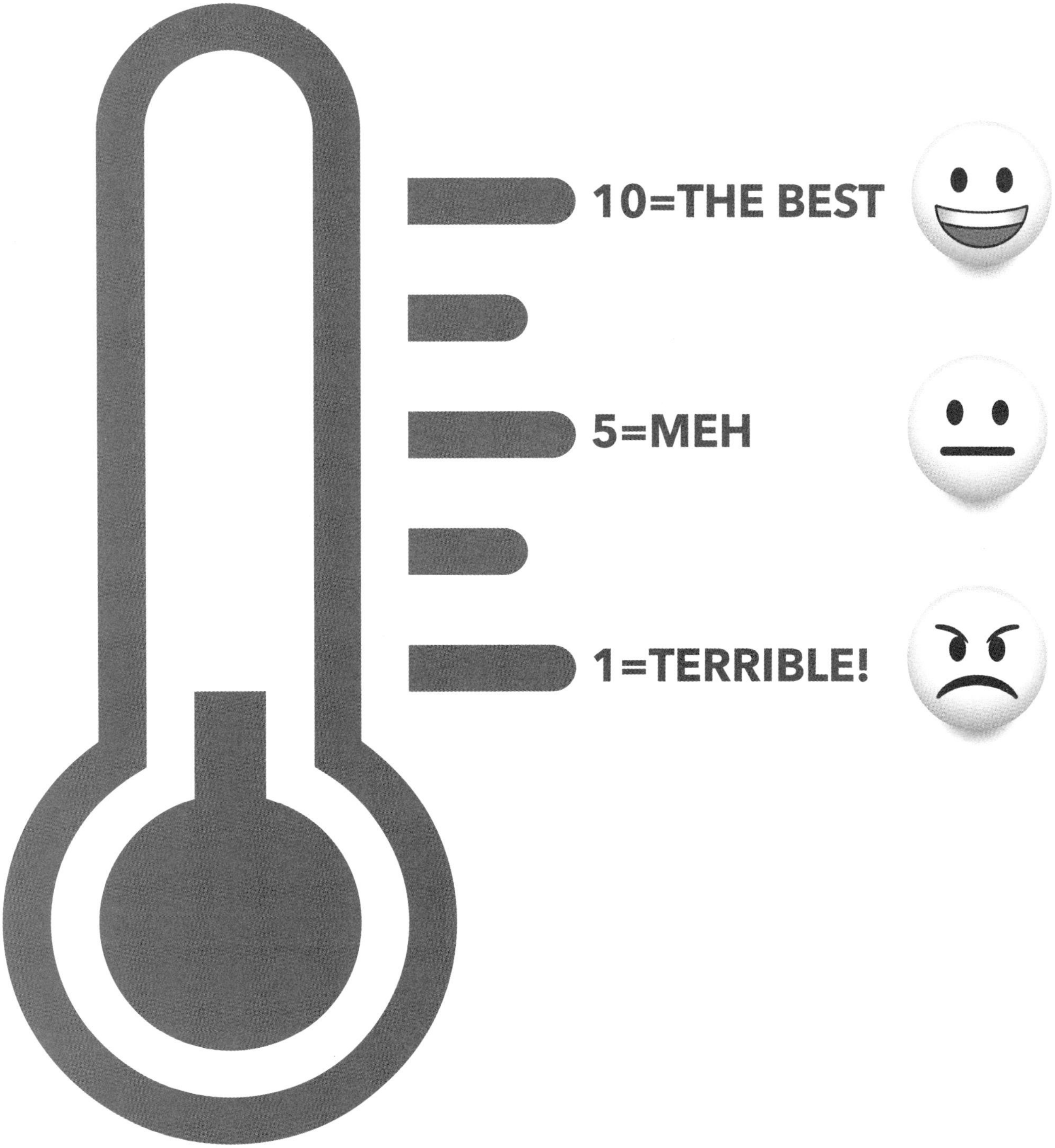

# Group Rules and Consequences

*Student Reproducible*

## GROUP RULES

1. Only say helpful comments.
2. Don't tell others what is said in the group.
3. One person talks at a time; there are no side conversations.
4. Use the bathroom before or after group only.
5. Name-calling is not allowed.
6. Don't touch someone else's stuff.
7. If you arrive late, bring a pass with the time/ an adult signature.

## CONSEQUENCES

1. Private Warning
2. Removal from Group

# Pre/Posttest

*Student Reproducible*

Name ______________________________ Date ______________

## The Support Cohort

| PRETEST | STATEMENTS | POSTTEST |
| --- | --- | --- |
| ❑ YES<br>❑ NO<br>❑ I DON'T KNOW | I can name all 5 characteristics of a SMART goal. | ❑ YES<br>❑ NO<br>❑ I DON'T KNOW |
| ❑ YES<br>❑ NO<br>❑ I DON'T KNOW | I can show someone how to do the grounding technique. | ❑ YES<br>❑ NO<br>❑ I DON'T KNOW |
| ❑ YES<br>❑ NO<br>❑ I DON'T KNOW | I know how to achieve my goals. | ❑ YES<br>❑ NO<br>❑ I DON'T KNOW |
| ❑ YES<br>❑ NO<br>❑ I DON'T KNOW | I am successful in school. | ❑ YES<br>❑ NO<br>❑ I DON'T KNOW |
| ❑ YES<br>❑ NO<br>❑ I DON'T KNOW | I can state five different positive coping habits that someone could use to feel better if they are having a bad week. | ❑ YES<br>❑ NO<br>❑ I DON'T KNOW |

# Growing with Grounding

*Student Reproducible*

Grounding is a relaxation technique that helps a person be mindful of their present moment. Studies have shown that spending time each day focusing on your present sensations can help improve mental health and reduce stress. In the grounding technique, a person thinks or talks about what they are experiencing at that exact moment with each of their five senses. Let's read the following instructions and then the counselor will model each one before we try them out for ourselves. It is fine to do this on your own or with a partner. After the activity, discuss your grounding experience with the group.

1. **Take a deep breath in through your nose and out through your mouth.**
2. **Focus your attention on three different things that you can see with your eyes and name each object out loud.**
3. **Now focus your attention on three different things you can smell with your nose and name them out loud.**
4. **Next, focus your attention on three things that you can taste with your mouth and name them out loud. (This could be a piece of food that you put on your tongue at the start of this activity or maybe just notice the taste that you already have in your mouth, like the toothpaste from brushing your teeth this morning.)**
5. **Next, focus your attention on three different things you can hear with your ears and name them out loud.**
6. **Finally, focus your attention on three different things you can touch with your hands and name them out loud.**
7. **To end this technique, take one more deep breath and bring your attention back to the group.**

GROUP SESSION 2

# Success with SMART Goals

## TOPIC OVERVIEW

**The group member will:**

- Continue building rapport with other group members
- Review group rules/norms
- Share their SMART goal success with the group
- Explore the grounding technique as a positive coping habit
- Identify various positive coping habits and illustrate their favorite one as a reminder to use it in difficult situations
- Apply the Miracle Question technique in a drawing to serve as another positive coping habit

**Materials**

- Reproducibles: The Miracle Illustration, Positive Coping Habits
- Items: photocopies of the goal note cards, crayons or markers, pencils, a healthy snack and some water for the grounding activity (if possible), construction paper
- Former Reproducibles (from session 1): Scaling Thermometer, Group Notes Sheet, Group Evaluation, Group Rules & Consequences

**Procedures**

1. Take attendance on the Group Notes sheet and offer students a Scaling Thermometer sheet to think about and color as a warmup. If necessary, review the meaning of scaling.
2. Lead the students in the Growing into Grounding technique from session one; this will get everyone relaxed and ready to focus on the group session.
3. Review the group rules by having each member read a rule aloud in a round robin fashion. Remind group members that they can say "pass" if they do not want to read aloud.
4. Have students share their scaling numbers and explain why they have picked that number. The scaling discussion is also a good time address any concerns students want to discuss related to the group theme, but make sure this scaling/discussion part doesn't exceed 10 minutes of the group time. If you gave counseling homework in the last session, have students share their homework experience at this time.
5. Hand out the photocopies of the goal note cards. Display the following Goal Success Sharing steps for members to reference in every group session:

   **GOAL SUCCESS SHARING STEPS**

   **1. Read your goal aloud.**
   **2. Give an example of your success with your goal.**

   Model how to do steps 1 and 2. For example, you can read off an imaginary note card: "My goal for being successful in school this week is to get a passing grade in my math class." Then you can tell the group the following imaginary success: "When I checked my grades with my teacher yesterday, I had a 66% in math, but I passed my math test yesterday so that is a success."

6. Give group members 1 minute to think of a success they had in the past week with their note card goal. **You may want to provide members with a computer printout of their class grades and/or discipline referral reports so they can check measurable data related to their goal.*

7. Allow each group member to present their goal success to the group.

8. Hand out the Positive Coping Habits reproducible and discuss the definition of positive coping habits. Read down the list with the group members in round robin fashion and explain any positive coping habits (PCH) that they don't understand. Pair up group members and have them tell their partner their favorite PCH and why. Students should then share their partner's PCH with the group.

9. Have students copy their preferred PCH onto the bottom of their goal note card so they remember what it is in order to reflect and apply it throughout the week. Collect the goal note cards. Photocopy the note cards after group and give group members a copy the following day as a reminder to work toward their SMART goal and practice their coping habit during the week. Keep the originals for the next group session.

10. Have members illustrate and color their favorite PCH and display them on the group room walls so that students will be reminded of their PCH each time they come to group. Briefly discuss drawing as a PCH and how they would use it during rough times at school or home. **If your group meeting area is not a confidential space, you will need to take down and re-display these drawings every session.*

11. If time, lead students in another PCH drawing activity, the Miracle Illustration.

12. Complete the group evaluation as in the previous session.

**Optional Homework Activity**

- Have group members practice their preferred PCH this week whenever they experience negative feelings. Tell them to carefully observe whether it is helpful or not in reducing their negative feeling. They will share their experiences with using their PCHs in the next session.

**Discussion Questions**

- Are you happy with your success so far towards your SMART goal? Why or why not?
- What PCH is still a bit confusing to you?
- Why did you choose the PCH you told your partner about as your favorite?
- How can PCHs help us to avoid emergencies and to achieve our SMART goals?

# Positive Coping Habits

*Student Reproducible*

Positive coping habits (PCH) are the repeated and consistent activities that people do to tolerate or reduce negative feelings or events. For example, if someone has bad memories of family violence that was resolved a few years ago, they might talk with a trusted friend to either distract themselves from these bad memories or to process the memories. The key is that PCHs do not harm a person's body or mind (such as fighting or abusing alcohol would if used as a distraction from negative thoughts or feelings); instead PCHs only work to make someone feel better. Below is a list of common PCHs that many people find effective to use. Throughout our group experience, we will practice using a different one in each session.

1. **Drawing**
   Example: Illustrate a day in your life when you didn't have any problems.

2. **Writing**
   Example: Write a funny story or a letter to your pet.
3. **Exercise**
   Example: Take a walk or a run through nature and enjoy the scenery. Even better, take your pet with you!
4. **Breath Work**
   Example: Try 3-5-7 breathing: inhale for a count of 3, hold for a count of 5, exhale for a count of 7.
5. **Coloring**
   Example: Create your own mandala and color it.
6. **Progressive Muscle Relaxation**
   Example: Lead yourself through a session of desk yoga while you are in class.
7. **Parasympathetic System Activation**
   Example: Use the self-hug or hand massage to trigger this system and help you calm down.
8. **Aromatherapy**
   Example: Put some scented lotion on your hands. Next, breathe in through your nose and out through your mouth to enjoy the calming effects of the pleasant aroma.
9. **"I" Message Communication**
   Example: Share your thoughts or feelings with another person by starting with the word "I".
10. **Help from A Trusted Adult**
    Example: Anytime someone might get physically hurt, tell an adult right away.

# The Miracle Illustration

*Student Reproducible*

How amazing would your life be if you woke up tomorrow and you had achieved every part of your goal?? Imagine that the problem hindering the goal was GONE!! Let's turn this "miracle" into a positive coping habit by drawing a picture of it. First, take a minute to let your imagination run wild and think about what your life would be like if this miracle occurs for you tonight. Next, in the box below, draw and color an image or scene representing this "miracle" taking place in your life. Once everyone is finished, we will do a Gallery Walk so group members can see and celebrate your miracle with you!

GROUP SESSION 3

# Nature and Exercise for the Win!

## TOPIC OVERVIEW

**The group member will:**

- Share their SMART goal success with the group
- Practice the grounding technique as a positive coping habit
- Incorporate nature and exercise into their collection of positive coping habits
- Explore how activating the parasympathetic system can work as a positive coping habit

**Materials**

- Reproducibles: The Natural Way, Give Yourself a Hand
- Items: photocopies of the goal note cards, crayons or markers, pencils, clipboards, a healthy snack and some water for the grounding activity (if possible)
- Former Reproducibles (from session 1): Scaling Thermometer, Group Notes Sheet, Group Evaluation, Group Rules & Consequences

**Procedures**

1. Take attendance on the Group Notes sheet and offer students a Scaling Thermometer sheet to think about and color as a warmup. If necessary, review the meaning of scaling.
2. Lead the students in the Growing into Grounding technique to get everyone relaxed and ready to focus on the group session.
3. Review the rules poster by having each group member read a rule aloud in a round robin fashion.
4. Have students share their scaling numbers and explain why they have picked that number. Also spend a few minutes discussing any concerns students want to address related to group theme. If you gave counseling homework in the last session, have students share their homework experience at this time.
5. Hand out the photocopies of the goal note cards. Choose a group member to model their goal success to serve as a reminder for group members that might have forgotten how to do this. Give group members a minute to think of a success they had in the past week with their note card goal. **You may want to provide members with a computer printout of their class grades and/or discipline referral reports so they can check measurable data related to their goal.*
6. Allow each group member to present their goal success to the group. Collect the goal note cards. Photocopy the note cards after group and give group members a copy the following day as a reminder to work toward their SMART goal and practice their positive coping habit (PCH) during the week. Keep the originals for the next group session.
7. Ask group members how nature and exercise might help someone to feel better if they are having a bad day. Guide them to the idea that both experiencing the natural world and engaging in exercise can release chemicals in the brain that calm us and make us feel better. Hand out The Natural Way reproducible and use it with students to experience another PCH.
8. If time, use the Give Yourself a Hand reproducible to lead students through a hand self-massage activity as another PCH in the form of a calming activity.
9. Complete the group evaluation as in the previous session.

**Optional Homework Activity**

- Teach a friend one of the positive coping habits that you learned today. Notice if they find the PCH calming and helpful or not.

**Discussion Questions**

- What did you most enjoy in today's session? Why?
- In your opinion, what is the main behavior that is helping or hindering your goal achievement?
- Today we learned about 3 different types of positive coping habits- exercise, spending time in nature, and the hand massage. Which do you feel is the most effective as a positive coping habit and why?

# The Natural Way

*Student Reproducible*

Did you know that both experiencing nature and engaging in exercise can release calming chemicals in the brain? This makes us feel better and function better, too! Let's experience this for ourselves by taking a group nature walk! During the walk, pay attention to how the outside elements (trees, grass, dirt, sand, rocks, bodies of water, clouds, birds, insects, etc.) make you feel. Also pay attention to how the physical act of walking makes you feel. On our nature walk, we will stop a few different times to reflect on our observations and jot down our thoughts and feelings about these observations. Use the chart below to record your walk experiences related to your 5 senses. Now place this sheet on a clipboard, take a pencil, and let's try out The Natural Way!!

## During the Walk

| | WHAT I EXPERIENCED/OBSERVED | HOW IT MADE ME FEEL |
|---|---|---|
| **Nature Sights** | | |
| **Nature Smells** | | |
| **Natural Sounds** | | |
| **Nature Objects I Touched** | | |
| **Moving My Body During the Walking Exercise** | | |

## After the Nature Walk

Now that the walk is over, let's discuss our experiences, observations, and feelings about it. Also, how might you incorporate a nature walk into your life at school or home? How would you use a nature walk in your life to raise your spirits if you are battling negative thoughts and feelings? (A nature walk can be an actual walk or a mental walk in your mind).

# Give Yourself a Hand!

*Student Reproducible*

Did you know that massaging your own hand can be an effective calming activity?!? It's true and it all relates to the parasympathetic system, which is the body system responsible for rest and digestion. Activating this system can help you to calm down if you are feeling over-energized with anger or stress. This is because there are nerves related to this system in the palm, so a palm self-massage can both trigger this system and increase a soothing blood flow to the muscles in the hand (Young et al., 2011). Let's try it by following the steps below!

1. **Hold out your left hand in front of you, palm up.**
2. **Place your right thumb in the middle of your left palm, with the other fingers of your right hand resting again the back of your left hand.**
3. **Use your right hand to squeeze your left hand in a rotating motion, with about 1 rotational squeeze per 2 seconds. Repeat this for 10 squeezes.**
4. **Switch hands so you are now massaging your right hand.**
5. **What did you think? Tell the group your opinion of this positive coping habit and if you felt that it calmed you.**

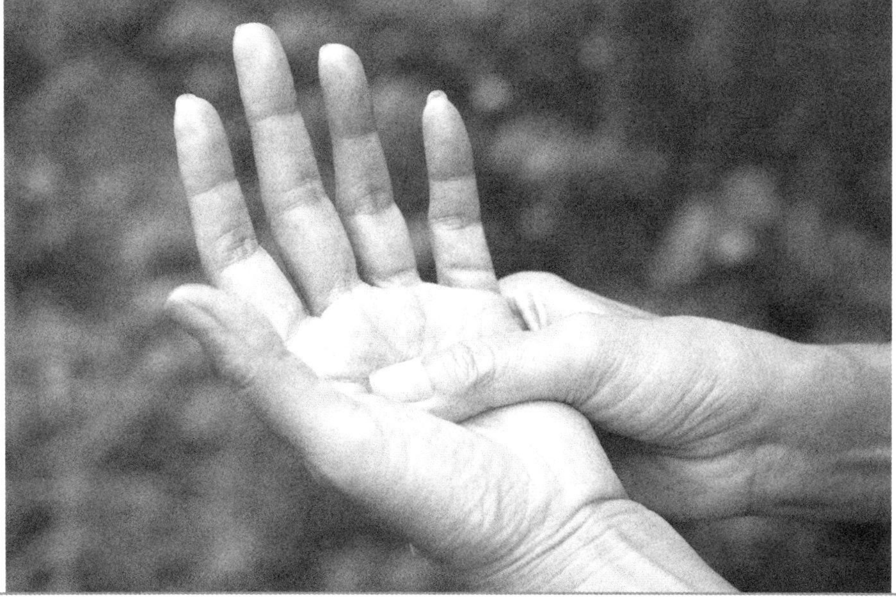

GROUP SESSION 4

# There's No "You" in "I" Message

## TOPIC OVERVIEW

**The group member will:**

- Share their SMART goal success with the group
- Practice the grounding technique as a positive coping habit
- Incorporate "I" messages into their collection of positive coping habits
- Explore how breath work can also be employed as a positive coping habit

**Materials**

- Reproducibles: There's No "You" in "I" Message, Breath Work, Interpersonal Problem Scenario Cards
- Items: photocopies of the goal note cards, crayons or markers, pencils, a healthy snack and some water for the grounding activity (if possible),
- Former Reproducibles (from session 1): Scaling Thermometer, Group Notes Sheet, Group Evaluation, Group Rules & Consequences

**Procedures**

1. Take attendance on the Group Notes sheet and offer students a Scaling Thermometer sheet to think about and color as a warmup.

2. Lead the students in the Growing into Grounding technique to get everyone relaxed and ready to focus on the group session.

3. Review the rules poster by having each group member read a rule aloud.

4. Have students share their scaling numbers and explain why they have picked that number. Briefly discuss any concerns students have related to the group theme. If you gave counseling homework in the last session, have students share their homework experience at this time.

5. Hand out the photocopies of the goal note cards and have group members share their goal success/es. Collect the goal note cards. For steps on how to share, use measurable data with, and reuse goal notes, see session 2.

6. Read the attached vignette from the There's No "You" in "I" Message to the group. Discuss how Sharon in the vignette solved her problem with Vanessa. Ask group members how solving an interpersonal problem calmly is a positive coping habit. Organize group members into pairs and give each member an interpersonal problem scenario and have them think about how to use an "I" message to solve the problem. Let pairs practice acting out their scenario with an "I" message and then perform this role play for the group. It is best for the counselor to model this role play process first.

7. If time, use the Breath Work reproducible to show students how to practice the 3-5-7 breath before giving an "I" message for especially challenging interpersonal problems.

8. Complete the group evaluation as in the previous session.

**Optional Homework Activity**

- Talk with a family member about your progress with your goal. Discuss your satisfaction or dissatisfaction on your own goal achievement. Get input from your relative on adding another goal if you are satisfied or revising your goal if you are unsatisfied.

**Discussion Questions**

- Why do you think the title of the first reproducible for this session is There's No "You" in "I" Message? (Guide students to the idea that the "I " message works because it withholds blame that can be inferred when someone starts a sentence with "You made me…" or "You didn't do…" or "You better stop…" Discuss how taking the "you" out of the problem communication and replacing it with "I" is a natural way to lessen negative feelings, thus helping to bring about a peaceful solution.)

- How did you feel while creating and acting out your "I" message role play?

- How is the 3-5-7 breath a PCH?

# There's No "You" in "I" Message

*Student Reproducible*

Interpersonal conflicts between people are a natural and normal part of human relationships. One of the best ways to peacefully solve an interpersonal conflict is to reduce the blame and negativity in discussing it. This is best done by calmly, yet firmly, beginning the resolution conversation with an "I" message. Let's take a look at the vignette below to see how this works. After, we will role play our own "I" messages in order to solve a problem.

## Vignette: Sharon VS. Vanessa

Sharon is mad at Vanessa because she feels like Vanessa is posting mean things about her on social media. Sharon wants this problem to stop, so she asks Vanessa if they can talk privately after school. When they meet at the bus stop, instead of yelling and pointing her finger in Vanessa's face, Sharon calmly states, "I am feeling hurt about something I saw that you posted on social media. Richard showed me on his social media account how you were saying that I only have one friend because I am annoying. Please don't write anything about me on social media." At this point, Vanessa grudgingly apologized and stormed off. Sharon knew they would probably not be friends again, but at least she had tried to solve the problem in the most peaceful way possible. It was hard to have that kind of conversation, but keeping her goal of ending the mean social media comments really helped Sharon find her courage. And she just kept reminding herself that her goal was not to make Vanessa like her or be her friend, but instead to end the nasty comments. And Voila! Her "I" message solution worked- there were no more mean comments after that! She did catch Vanessa throwing a few ugly looks her way from time to time, but hey, Sharon had no issue with someone who couldn't control their own immature facial expressions. All's well that ends well!

### Vignette Process Discussion

- How did Sharon in the vignette use an "I" message to solve her problem of Vanessa writing mean things about her on social media?
- Do you feel like the "I" message worked to solve Sharon's problem?
- What would you do if you were in Sharon's position? Vanessa's position? Richard's position?
- How is solving an interpersonal problem calmly a PCH?

### "I" Message Role Play Steps

1. Organize yourself into pairs.
2. Take an interpersonal problem scenario card and read it with your partner.
3. Discuss how to use an "I" message to solve the problem on your card.
4. With your partner, practice acting out your scenario to solve the problem with an "I" message.
5. Finally, perform your "I" message role play for the group.

# Interpersonal Problem Scenario Cards

*Student Reproducible*

| | |
|---|---|
| On the ride to my grandparent's house, my brother always gets to hold the dog. I never get to have the dog sit on my lap during the car ride. | My dad thinks that it is funny to startle me by sneaking up behind me and yelling "Boo!" in my ear. I am sixteen for heaven's sake! I am too old for this game and it really scares me. I hate it when he does this. |
| My sister always runs to the car to be the one to ride in the front seat. Sometimes I'd like to sit in the front seat. | The girl who sits near me in math class keeps giving me mean looks. It is really upsetting me. |
| My best friend calls me Big Chungus. I know he means it in a funny way because he loves this chubby cartoon character, but it really hurts my feelings. | This summer, the neighborhood kids and I are putting on a production of the musical play, Annie. Unfortunately, they always make me play the part of Sandy, the dog. I don't want to be the dog. I want a lead role. |
| The new guy who just started at my middle school is trying to take all my friends away from me by telling everyone rumors about me. | At recess, Jeremy always throws the dodgeball right at my face. I want to keep playing in the game, but I can't keep taking these cheek hits. |
| The math teacher jokes with me too much, so I can't concentrate. I know she thinks I am so smart that I can handle the distraction, but it is really starting to bother me. | My former BFF is now talking mess about me to everyone since we had a big argument. I really need her to stop or there's going to be a fight. |

# Breath Work

*Student Reproducible*

If an interpersonal conflict between two people is especially challenging or frustrating, it can be helpful to take a few moments to do some breath work. Calming yourself with the 3-5-7 breath is not only a calming positive coping habit, but it can give you the time and clarity to express your thoughts with an "I" message. Let's try out the 3-5-7 breath now.

INSTRUCTIONS:

1. **Breath in through your nose while counting "1-Mississippi, 2-Mississippi, 3-Mississippi".**

2. **Hold your breath for a "1-Mississippi..." etc. count up to 5.**

3. **Breathe out through pursed lips while counting "1-Mississippi..." etc. until you get to 7.**

4. **Repeat 2 more times.**

GROUP SESSION 5

# Positive Coping Habits at Your Desk

## TOPIC OVERVIEW

**The group member will:**

- Share their SMART goal success with the group
- Practice the grounding technique as a positive coping habit
- Learn various progressive muscle relaxation techniques that they can utilize at their desk in the classroom
- Explore how coloring and artistic expression can also be used as a positive coping habit

**Materials**

- Reproducibles: Yoga, Make Your Own Mandala
- Items: photocopies of the goal note cards, crayons or markers, pencils, paper, a healthy snack and some water for the grounding activity (if possible)
- Former Reproducibles (from session 1): Scaling Thermometer, Group Notes Sheet, Group Evaluation, Group Rules & Consequences

**Procedures**

1. Take attendance on the Group Notes sheet and offer students a Scaling Thermometer sheet to think about and color as a warmup.
2. Lead the students in the Growing into Grounding technique to get everyone relaxed and ready to focus on the group session.
3. Review the rules poster by having each group member read a rule aloud.
4. Have students share their scaling numbers and explain why they have picked that number. This 5-10 minute scaling discussion is also a good time address any concerns students want to address related to group theme. Discuss with the group that the next session will be the last scheduled session; let them know that they can meet with you individually on an as-needed basis and give them the procedures for requesting this type of meeting. In addition, ask them whether they would like a follow-up group session in one month and, if so, schedule it. See the recommendations section at the beginning of this guide for tips and content suggestions for the follow-up session.
5. If you gave counseling homework in the last session, have students share their homework experience at this time.
6. Hand out the photocopies of the goal note cards and have group members share their goal success/es. Collect the goal note cards. For steps on how to share, use measurable data with, and reuse goal notes, see session 2.
7. Use the attached reproducible Desk Yoga to teach the group members another positive coping habit (PCH) that utilizes progressive muscle relaxation.
8. If time, lead the students in another creative PCH where they will create and color their own mandalas as a calming technique. Follow the steps in Make Your Own Mandala to guide students through this activity.
9. Complete the group evaluation as in the previous session.

# Positive Coping Habits at Your Desk

*(continued)*

**Optional Homework Activity**

- Try out some desk yoga the next time you have a test or a stressful moment in class. Notice how it makes you feel in your mind and in your body. We will discuss your observations and experience in our next session.

**Discussion Questions**

- How do you feel when you solve a problem?
- Tell us about a time you solved a problem in your life.
- How do you think the act of solving a problem could help someone feel better overall about a bad event or memory in their life?

# Desk Yoga

*Student Reproducible*

*When we feel stress and anxiety, we often hold that stress in our body by tensing up our muscles. This causes all kinds of aches and pains. One way to reduce this tension and also calm yourself so you don't clench up your muscles in the future is through progressive muscle relaxation, or PMR. PMR is a physical activity where you clench and release a group of muscles. If you combine this PMR with breath work at your desk, you can turn it into desk yoga!! Follow the steps below to try it now and see how it makes you feel.*

## DESK YOGA STEPS

1. Find a comfortable and slightly relaxed position in your chair at your desk, sitting upright with your forearms on your desk and your feet on the floor about 6 inches apart.

2. Begin this activity with 3 deeps breaths–in through your nose and out through pursed lips.

3. Complete each desk yoga position below by following the descriptions.

   - **CHAIR STRETCH LEFT**
     Bend your left arm at the elbow and lay it over the back of your chair. Turning your torso slightly to the left, grab the back-left side of your chair with your right hand. Both feet should stay on the ground, or at least be facing forward if your feet don't touch the ground. Hold for 5 seconds tensing your shoulder muscles slightly, release your muscles that are holding you to this position, and return to facing front. Repeat 2 more times.

   - **CHAIR STRETCH RIGHT**
     Bend your right arm at the elbow and lay it over the back of your chair. Turning your torso slightly to the right, grab the back-right side of your chair with your left hand. Both feet should stay on the ground, or at least facing forward if your feet don't touch the ground. Hold for 5 seconds tensing your shoulder muscles slightly, release your muscles that are holding you to this position, and return to facing front. Repeat 2 more times.

   - **THE STRING**
     Slide to the edge of your chair and sit comfortably with your feet on the floor and your arms at your side. Your back should not be touching your chair. Now imagine that there is a wire connected to your spine and coming out of the top of your head- imagine that the wire is being pulled taut from the ceiling, pulling your back and head into a straight line with it. Sit straight like this for a few seconds, feeling your back and abdominal muscles clenching. Now release and relax those muscles. Repeat 2 more times.

# Desk Yoga

*Student Reproducible*

*(continued)*

- **REACH FOR THE STARS**
  Continuing to sit in your straight-backed wire-from-the-head position, slowly raise your arms up above your head, palms facing each other. Stretch your arms towards the ceiling and then lean back in your chair slightly; feel those arm muscles clench as you reach for the stars. Gently return to sitting straight and lower your arms, releasing those clenched muscles. Repeat 2 more times.

- **THE ARCH**
  Continue sitting at the edge of your chair and reach back with both hands to hold the back-bottom seat edge of your chair. Now slowly arch your back and look at the ceiling, feeling the muscles in your back tighten. Only arch as far as is comfortable. Return to sitting straight. Repeat 2 more times.

- **THE BEND**
  Now slide back in your chair as far as you can, until your back is touching the back of your chair. Keep your feet flat on the floor and bend over as far as you can until your stomach is on your thighs. Drop your head and arms towards the floor and let them relax to hang down. Hold the position for a few seconds and then gently and slowly return to sitting upright position. Repeat 2 more times.

4. Now sit upright again in your chair and end this activity with 3 more deeps breaths–in through your nose and out through pursed lips.

## PROCESSING DESK YOGA

Talk with your group members about how these desk yoga poses made you feel. If you liked this activity, there are lots more yoga positions you can learn about and try out at **Kidshealth.com**!!

# Make Your Own Mandala

*Student Reproducible*

*Coloring is a very soothing activity for many people. It promotes mindfulness because you have to focus all your attention on the present tasks of choosing colors, staying inside the lines, etc. Mandalas are designs that represent the universe in certain religions; the word mandala means center or circle in Sanskrit. Many people enjoy coloring mandalas and find filling them in with bursts of color to be a relaxing activity. You can find mandalas all over the internet, but did you know you can also make your own? Follow the steps below to create and color your own mandala!*

## STEPS

1. Starting at the top of your paper draw a big circle in pencil.
2. As you are finishing the circle, make a line down the center of the circle to its other side without taking your pencil off the paper.
3. Once you get to the other side of the circle, start filling in the center of the circle by drawing all kinds of lines and squiggles, intersecting and crossing over each other, without ever taking your pencil off the paper. Do this for 15 seconds.
4. Now you have created your mandala and you are ready to color it in! Enjoy!!

## GALLERY WALK & TALK

Leave your mandala out on your desk area for others to observe. Walk around the room, noticing others' mandalas and how their bursts of color make you feel. Once the Gallery Walk is over, discuss this activity with your group members. How did it make you feel? Was it relaxing? Did it make you practice mindfulness (focusing only on the present experience)? How could creating and coloring a mandala be a PCH?

GROUP SESSION 6

# The Final Countdown

## TOPIC OVERVIEW

**The group member will:**

- Share their SMART goal success with the group
- Practice the grounding technique as a positive coping habit
- Explore writing and aromatherapy as additional positive coping habits
- Reflect on their experiences with the group
- Evaluate the group experience

**Materials**

- Reproducibles: Put it in Writing, Group Experience Evaluation
- Items: photocopies of the goal note cards, chart paper, blank note cards, crayons or markers, paper, pencils, a healthy snack and some water for the grounding activity (if possible)
- Former Reproducibles (from session 1): Scaling Thermometer, Group Notes Sheet, Rules & Consequences, Pre/Posttest

**Procedures**

**This final session tends to run long, taking as long as 90 minutes to complete. If you don't have the extra time needed for this session, consider omitting the scaling, grounding, discussion, and homework shareout activities in order to save time.*

1. Take attendance on the Group Notes sheet and offer students a Scaling Thermometer sheet to think about and color as a warmup.
2. Lead the students in the Growing into Grounding technique to get everyone relaxed and ready to focus on the group session.
3. Review the rules poster by having each group member read a rule aloud.
4. Have students share their scaling numbers and explain why they have picked that number. If necessary, allow students to address any concerns related to group theme. If you are ending the group with this session, remind group members that this is the last group session, and briefly discuss plans for the follow-up session, if you will be having one.
5. If you gave counseling homework in the last session, have students share their homework experience at this time.
6. Hand out the photocopies of the goal note cards and have group members share their goal success/es. If anyone wants to add a second SMART goal, allow some time for this. Group members can take their note cards home with them today unless you need to make photocopies for a follow-up session.
7. Review with group members all the main points learned during these sessions. To facilitate this, have each group member share 1-2 main points they learned in group. They can do this sharing in a round robin format. Write their ideas on the board or on chart paper.
8. Hand out the pretest/posttest (from session 1) and read it aloud as group members fill in Yes/No for each posttest statement. Make sure group members write answers in the posttest column and don't change any of their pretest answers. Collect and save the completed posttests for data purposes.

9. Complete the Group Experience Evaluation. To do this, read each evaluation statement aloud while the group members write down their response to that statement. Collect and retain the completed evaluations for data purposes.

10. Give students a final protective factor to add to their positive coping habits toolbox. Use the attached reproducible, Put it in a Letter, to lead students through a writing activity that promotes reflection and closure; group members who have experienced trauma will find this especially helpful since the group (a major protective factor in itself) is ending. **If your group members are very young or are non-writers, have them draw their responses to the writing prompt instead, illustrating the main points as in a comic strip.*

11. Consider adding an aromatherapy element to this writing activity by placing a basket in the center of the group table with various scented items such as lotion, stickers, and crayons or markers. Briefly discuss with students that pleasant smells can serve as a PCH for some people because they can improve mood and lessen anxiety (Cleveland Clinic, 2015). Encourage the students to use one or all of the aromatherapy tools as they write, illustrate, and decorate their story or letter. If possible, allow some time at the end of the activity for students to experience the calming effects of aromatherapy by leading them in a breathing exercise: have them breathe in through their nose to smell the scent and then out through their mouth to expel any negative or anxious feelings from their body.

12. Praise the group members for all of their hard work. Ask whether there is anything more they would like to discuss or any other help they need. Remind them to let you know if they need to meet with you anytime in the future.

**If your group members are very young or struggle with writing, consider reducing the number of items in steps 8/9 and having students dictate their responses to you.*

**Optional Homework Activity**

- Share your closure writing piece with a friend or family member. Ask them about a time in their life when they needed closure for something important that ended.

**Discussion Questions**

- How do you feel now that the group has ended?
- Did the writing/aromatherapy activity help you to experience closure at all? Why or why not?
- How do you feel overall about your progress with your goal achievement now that the group is over?

# Put it in Writing

*Student Reproducible*

As our group comes to a close, it is time to reflect on our experiences here in order to give ourselves closure. Closure is the process by which people understand and accept an ending as a normal and inevitable part of life, even though it may make them sad. In this final group session, we will celebrate the positive aspects of our group experience by telling about them in one of the following ways.

<u>DIRECTIONS</u>

Choose one of the prompts below and write a one-page story or letter about it. Just do your best, the idea is to enjoy the process of reflecting on the group experience. Writing conventions such as handwriting and grammar are not important for this activity; only your ideas matter here. After you have finished writing, you can use crayons, markers, and crafty items (glitter, tissue paper, yarn, stickers, etc.) to illustrate your story and/or decorate it. If there is time once everyone has finished writing, we will take a Gallery Walk to observe and reflect on each other's closure pieces.

## WRITING PROMPTS

- **Write about a funny story or event that occurred in this group.**
- **Write a letter to your pet about what the group experience was like for you.**

# Group Experience Evaluation

*Student Reproducible*

Congratulations on completing this Support Cohort group program! Employing positive coping habits and achieving goals is hard work, but the end result of feeling and functioning better is absolutely worth it!! Please take a few minutes now to reflect on what you've learned in group and then answer the following questions.

1. **What have you learned about yourself through our group experience?**

2. **Would you recommend this group to a friend? Why or why not?**

3. **Which group activity did you find most useful? Least useful?**

4. **What did you learn about other members of the group during the group experience?**

5. **Describe 3 positive coping habits you have learned in this group.**

**ADDITIONAL COMMENTS:**

# Additional Activities

*Counselor Information Sheet & Instruction Sheet*

As mentioned in the recommendations section, these are additional activities for extending your sessions. These activities have been created to extend the group counseling experience past the 6 sessions that are provided in this book. In addition, these activities can be added into existing sessions if you'd like to extend the length of your group sessions past one hour. You can also substitute any of the additional activities for a particular session activity if that activity won't work with your group members.

## SELF-HUG

Like the hand massage strategy of session 4, the self-hug is another effective calming activity. Hugs of any kind, whether received from ourselves or another person, can trigger the release of oxytocin. Research shows that an increase in the chemical oxytocin can trigger feelings of calm and safety (Neff, 2020). Have your students try this out to get their happy chemicals flowing! First, ask students to stand and cross their arms in front of their body to reach around and grasp the backs of their shoulders- right hand grasping left shoulder and left hand grasping right shoulder. They should then squeeze and hold the hug for a count of 5. Next have students release, letting their arms gently drop to their sides. Repeat 2 more times. Wrap up this activity with a brief discussion to process the self-hug: How did it make them feel? Why do they think it might work as a calming activity? How it is a positive coping habit?

## STOPLIGHT

Stoplight is a simple interpersonal problem-solving activity that is very effective in getting students to deescalate and solve a conflict, rather than ramping it up to a more serious level. This activity is a must-do for a few minutes in every session if students are having interpersonal conflicts with others. To begin, show students the following stoplight posterette and explain each step or "light" of solving a conflict. Have students color each of the three stoplight boxes their correct color according to the bolded word to the right of the box. Next have students practice each of the stoplight colors in pairs using a conflict card/scenario, with the counselor modeling this first. Finally, discuss with the group which steps were the most difficult and how thinking of this activity could help them through future interpersonal conflicts.

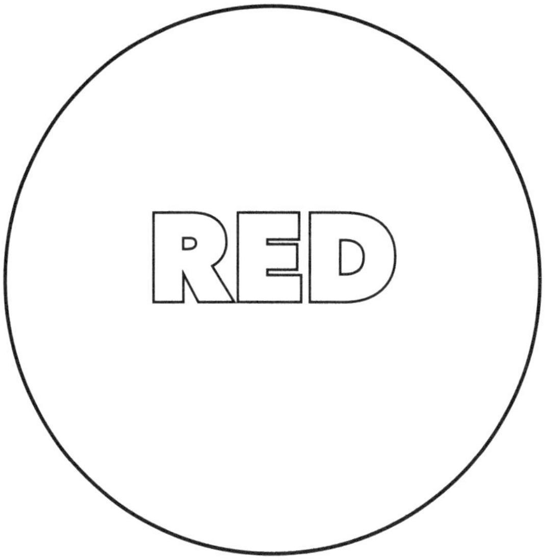


**Red** means you are too angry or upset to think clearly. Remove yourself from the conflict (for example- walk away, block on social media, ask for a break alone, etc.) and practice a positive coping habit that you think will best calm you down so you can think clearly.

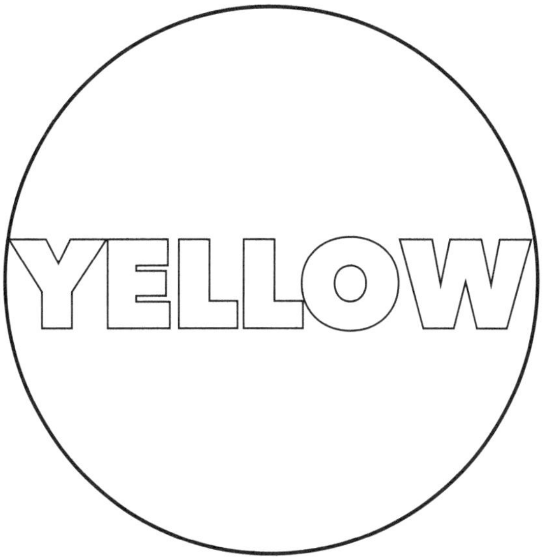


**Yellow** means that the conflict is still there, but you have calmed down enough to think through how to solve it. Pick a solution from your positive coping habits list (session 2) that you think will best solve this conflict.

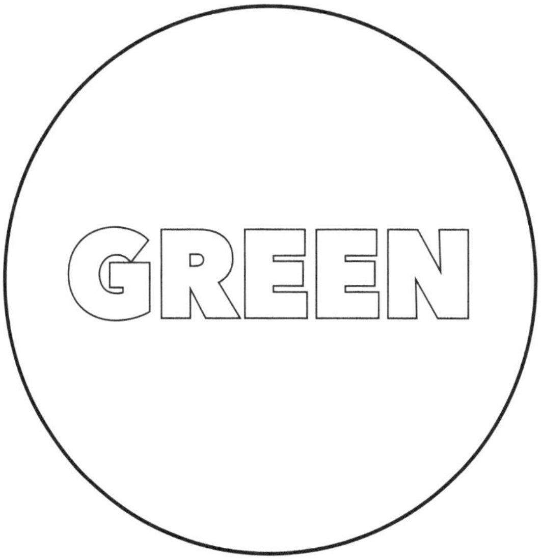


**Green** means that you have your solution and you are ready to try it out to solve the conflict. If it works, great! If not, head back to yellow and select a different solution.

| | |
|---|---|
| Hector keeps hugging you even though you don't want him to. | Your English teacher gave you a "D" on your midterm paper that you didn't deserve. |
| Larry and Jorge are arguing loudly and you can't concentrate on your math work. | Your best friend used to give you a ride to school every day, but now she doesn't want to. |
| Elisa steals some candy out of your backpack and eats it at lunch. | You and your neighbor used to play basketball after school, but now he's too busy with his new girlfriend to make any time for you. |
| Your mom tells you to stop making the dog bark even though your brother is the one doing it. | Jennifer and Jessica are ganging up on you at recess, calling you names and making fun of you. |

## FREEFORM DODGE BALL

This is a wonderful activity from the TBRI world on building self-regulation in students. For this activity, you will need to get a foam ball for each group member. Carefully explain that the purpose of the game is to have some fun playing freeform dodge ball, but that there are two crucial rules to this game. First, group members can never throw the ball at another group member's face. Second, they must always ask permission before throwing the ball at someone; if the receiving group member says "no" to a throw, the thrower must respect that and move on (Purvis, 2013). Take the students outside and allow them to play for about 10 minutes. After the game, collect all foam balls and sit everyone in a circle to process the activity- how did they feel while throwing and getting "hit" with the foam balls? how difficult was it to remember to ask permission before throwing?, etc.

## BIBLIO-COUNSELING

If you have any of my other counseling books, you know that I love biblio-counseling! Using books to engage group members and give them insight into their struggles is very effective in a trauma-informed group. Since "less is more" for some groups of this nature, I didn't include biblio-counseling into every session. Last year I ran a group like this that wasn't flowing smoothly until I cut out the biblio-counseling and homework activities to shorten each session by 15 minutes; it was just what they needed and the sessions flowed much more smoothly after I made this change. However, if you have a group that can handle a lengthier session, feel free to include a biblio-counseling element into every session. To do this, begin by introducing the book to the group, taking guesses on what it might be about based on the title and cover pictures. Then, read some of the story aloud in each session and relate the events of the story back to what students are learning in group; you can do this through questions such as:

- > What is the problem in the story? How does it relate to a problem we've discussed in group?
- > What positive coping habits have you noticed in the story? What about unhealthy coping habits?
- > Did you like the story? Why or why not?

## BOUNCING FORWARD

Grit and resilience are important topics to address with all students, and especially those who have experienced trauma. Here is a simple, yet effective idea to facilitate these concepts. Tell students that everyone faces challenges and rough times at some point in their lives. Discuss that it takes grit and resilience to overcome these challenges. Define these two terms with the students and then ask them to interview a family member or family friend who has used grit and resilience to "bounce forward" and overcome a challenge in their life. Have students jot down some notes or draw a picture of their family member's experience and share in it a future session. Make sure the students get interviewee permission to share.

# Data Analysis

*Counselor Instructions & Information*

**PART 1- GROUP DESCRIPTION**

**Explanation: In this part, include the title of the group, the semester and year it occurred, the total number of group members, and a brief description of the group.**

**SAMPLE**

The Support Cohort, Fall ______
Total Number of Group Members: 6
The Support Cohort is a group for students who struggle with various life experiences and/or finding success in school. Group members learn positive coping habits as well as how to set a goal and achieve it. Students continue in the group for 6-8 sessions. We also use group techniques such as discussion, role plays, games, and more to help them achieve their goals.

**PART 2- GROUP MEMBER EVALUATIONS**

**Explanation: In this part, include a brief summary of the student evaluation instrument and some meaningful group member evaluation quotes showing what they learned in group.**

**SAMPLE**

Students complete a short evaluation during our final group session to evaluate the group experience–what went well, what didn't go well, how the group has helped them, what they still need help with, etc.
Student responses:

*As a result of the group, I learned...*

- *good coping habits.*
- *that my thoughts are what make me angry and that I can control my anger if I try.*
- *that when I have problems, I know how to get help.*
- *that other group members help me calm down and make me happy.*
- *we all have family issues.*

**PART 3- PRE/POSTTEST RESULTS**

**Explanation: In this part, compile the group members' pre/posttest answers into the chart below, using an Excel spreadsheet. Then highlight the chart in Excel, click on the "Insert" tab in the ribbon of commands, click on "Insert Column Chart," and select the first 2-D Column Chart option; this automatically turns the chart into a graph. Once the graph has been created, you can customize it using one of the design options Excel offers; keep it easy and simple by using layout 9 from the "Quick Layout" pulldown menu under "Chart Tools > Design." See sample below.**

**SAMPLE CHART**

| | S1-SMART GOALS | S2-MINDFULNESS | S3-GOAL ACHIEVEMENT | S4- SCHOOL SUCCESS | S5-POSITIVE COPING HABITS |
|---|---|---|---|---|---|
| PRETEST: NUMBER OF CORRECT (AFFIRMATIVE) ANSWERS | 0 | 2 | 4 | 0 | 1 |
| POSTTEST: NUMBER OF CORRECT (AFFIRMATIVE) ANSWERS | 5 | 6 | 6 | 5 | 6 |

**SAMPLE BAR GRAPH**

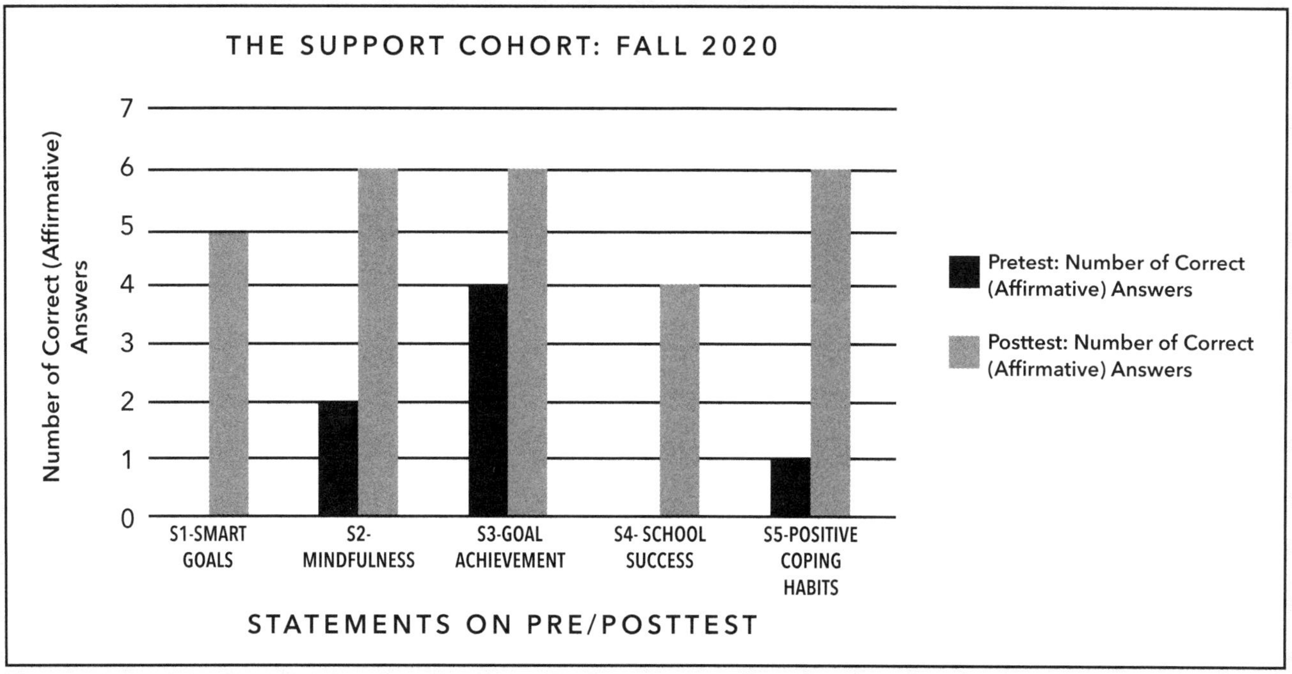


**PART FOUR- GOAL ACHIEVEMENT**

**Explanation: In this part, analyze the SMART goals that the students chose for themselves in the first group session, using data to determine if they achieved their SMART goal during the course of the group experience.**

**SAMPLE**

| | STUDENT GOAL | DATA POINT | GOAL ACHIEVED |
|---|---|---|---|
| Student 1 | My goal for being successful in school this week is to walk away from the problem and then get help from an adult. | No discipline referrals in **Term 2** | Yes |
| Student 2 | My goal for being successful in school this week is to keep my hands to myself. | No discipline referrals in **Term 2** | Yes |
| Student 3 | My goal for being successful in school this week is to pass my math class. | Passed math in **Term 2** report card | Yes |
| Student 4 | My goal for being successful in school this week is to use respectful language with peers and teachers. | 4 discipline referrals for profanity in **Term 2** | No |
| Student 5 | My goal for being successful in school this week is to take time out and relax and think it's no big deal (when I get mad). | No discipline referrals in **Term 2** | Yes |
| Student 6 | My goal for being successful in school this week is to complete my homework every night. | No homework zeroes in **Term 2** | Yes |

*The chart above shows that 83% of the group members achieved their SMART goal.*

**PART FIVE: ACADEMIC, ATTENDANCE, DISCIPLINE, OR CRISIS DATA**

**Explanation: Consider using similar types of Excel templates to compile data on grades, discipline referrals, absences, and/or crisis incidents of group members. Analyze group member data in the terms before, during, and after the counseling sessions. This will show how the group experience has contributed to various success-in-school factors such as decreased discipline referrals and increased attendance.**

**PART SIX- SUMMARY OF DATA**

**Explanation: In this part, we analyze all the charts and graphs in parts 3-5 and write a summary that explains the data trends for campus stakeholders.**

**SAMPLE**

The bar graph shows that the Support Cohort group members learned a lot on almost all of the pre/posttest topics, which reflected the main points covered in the group experience. In addition, 83% of the group members achieved their self-chosen grade/discipline goal. This shows the overwhelming success of the group sessions, since one of the main points of the group was to guide members to achieve their self-chosen success-in-school goal. It was mainly through the careful practice of various positive coping habits that students were able to focus less on their personal struggles and more on their school success.

***Our capacity to destroy one another is matched by our capacity to heal one another. Restoring relationships and community is central to restoring well-being.***

Dr. Bessel van der Kolk, *The Body Keeps the Score*

# Our Crisis Story

One of the reasons I decided to write this book is because, for years, I watched our school and district numbers of student *crisis rise, as the same was happening nationwide. I read everything I could get my hands on and went to countless crisis workshops to try to find a way to bring these numbers down at my school. But it turns out that finding a tool or solution that consistently decreases crisis numbers and increases student safety is like finding a unicorn! And, of course, these student crises were often linked to the trauma that students had experienced. Dr. Bruce Perry addresses this link by noting that self-harm "releases brain opioids, which makes it especially attractive to those who have been previously traumatized and found relief in dissociation… the experience [of self-harm] is far more likely to be perceived as pleasurable and attractive to those who have a **sensitized dissociation response from previous trauma and are in emotional pain" (Perry, 2017, p. 211). Moreover, Dr. Nadine Burke of the *Center for Youth Wellness*, adds to this crisis-trauma link by stating that toxic stress occurs "when a child experiences strong, frequent, and/or prolonged adversity—such as abuse or neglect—without adequate adult support" (Burke, 2018, p. 54). This can create a body situation where the "the amygdala alarm [is] always on high alert and the cortisol thermostat [is] overheating" (Burke, 2018, p. 185) which often leads directly to crisis situations.

So, what to do?!?! Well, when I couldn't find the crisis solutions I was looking for, I started figuring out how to create them myself. This led me to pitch a new angle to my colleagues and principal: the idea of starting every guidance lesson with a short mini-lesson on crisis identification, intervention, and prevention. That fall I piloted the idea and by the following year all counselors at my school were starting their guidance lessons in this manner. Imagine our joy and shock when we finally saw our numbers of student crisis outcries come down. This trend continued and even improved as we fine-tuned these crisis prevention mini-lessons. The grand finale came last year in late May when we ran the numbers and realized our student crisis outcries were down over 50% from the previous year!

So the moral of my little story above is that struggling students, especially those who have experienced trauma, are at great risk of having a crisis. Counselors can reduce this crisis risk greatly by including crisis identification and prevention strategies in every guidance lesson in the form of positive coping habits. In addition, all students benefit when a school success strategy is added into every guidance lesson—either as the focus of the entire lesson or as a quick 10-minute minilesson. Since research shows that academic success and coping skills are protective factors for the effects of trauma (CDC, 2009), every guidance lesson in Overcoming Strife in Life will include a positive coping habit for crisis prevention, as well as a school success strategy. The following section includes recommendations for setting up these lessons.

**Student crisis—physical harm to self or others*
***A sensitized dissociation response is a psychological reaction where someone is more likely to disconnect from their thoughts, feelings, memories or sense of identity.*

# General Information

- Overcoming Strife in Life contains 9 lesson plans for each month of the school year, starting with September and ending in May. If your students also attend school in June, July, and/or August- you can implement the assessment activities during these two months complemented by some additional activities provided at the end of this guidance curriculum. The focus of this guidance curriculum is on school success strategies and crisis prevention strategies that target positive coping habits and wellness. After this implementation section, a lesson plan for each month is provided with the accompanying reproducible worksheets and resources needed for that lesson. Most of the reproducibles reinforce these proactive strategies and are created for the student unless they specifically say "Counselor Information & Instructions". At the end of the guidance curriculum, additional activities are provided for extending your curriculum, if necessary.

- This guide has various, leveled activities making it appropriate for use with children in grades 3 through high school.

- This curriculum was developed for use in a school setting, but it can easily be modified for use in a clinical, or even virtual, setting.

- These lessons can be easily modified for the distance learning or virtual classroom by videoing yourself teaching the lesson and then uploading your video, as well as the lesson materials, into your school's FERPA- compliant online platform. Have students watch the video and then do the activities provided below for each lesson step. In addition, feel free to skip or modify the interactive parts that do not work for your specific distance learning environment, such as the January snowball throw; instead you might substitute in a biblio-counseling activity or one of the additional activities at the end of this guidance curriculum. Alternately, you can use Google Hangouts Meet or another online platform to actually simulate your guidance lesson classroom, where the class meets with you in real time as you teach the lesson. Here is a link to info about this platform and how to set it up:
**https://teachercenter.withgoogle.com/first-day-trainings/welcome-to-google-hangouts-meet**
*(Note: online platforms will change over time as do websites)*

- Here are some additional tips for modifying the lessons for distance learning.
  - Pair/group work can be done by having one pair practice at time or by assigning the group work as homework to be done with a family member; then students can share their home practice experience through a writing summary or verbally in the next lesson. This would work well with various activities such as the school success bingo game or with the October conflict resolution role play.

  - Reproducibles such as pre/posttests and final evaluations can be completed by uploading them to your online platform and then adding editing fields to the reproducibles, if your online platform has this capability; if not, you can have students complete reproducibles through an online comments/Q&A feature or simply by having students email their images/responses to you.

  - For the Scaling and/or Informal Lesson Evaluations, if students can't respond by holding up fingers or with a thumbs up/down response to each question, have them instead jot down their answers with a simple "yes/no" and submit them to you.

  - Consider having students do the school organization checklists with a family member as their accountability partner. Additionally, they can find answers by asking family members about their own social-emotional experiences. (For example, they might process February's Nike "Failure" video with a family member, rather than with a discussion in class.)

  - Encourage students to creatively find certain session materials in their own homes that they can use in the lesson–for example, students can use pebbles in their yard as bingo chips.

  - Direct students to use the internet to research lesson topics where it is too difficult for you to communicate the information they need in a distance learning environment.

  - Finally, feel free to remove any activities that don't flow as well in the virtual setting. The key in facilitating guidance lessons in the virtual setting is flexibility; with a bit of patience and tweaking, trauma-informed guidance lessons can run just as effectively in both types of settings.

- Keep in mind that this is a whole class guidance curriculum. It should be used to educate students on school success and wellness information. It should not be used as a substitute for mental health therapy with a licensed practitioner.

- Toxic stress is a very real problem that we are all dealing with nowadays, and our students are no exception! Toxic stress is the "result of a disruption to the stress response" (Burke, 2018, p. 171). There are five main ways to combat toxic stress: exercise, nutrition, mindfulness, mental health, and healthy relationships; these five life habits reduce stress hormones, reduce inflammation, and delay aging (Burke, 2018). As a result, you will see all of them built into this guide's crisis prevention resources.

- In keeping with the solution focused brief counseling (SFBC) theme of this book, there are a lot of SFBC activities in this guidance curriculum. Throughout the lessons, you'll see goal work, cheerleading, scaling, reflecting feelings, and detailing/coping questions.

- These lessons are also full of proactive strategies which serve as preventative teaching measures, and thus consist of "verbal reminders, behavioral rehearsals, role play with others or puppets, teaching life value terms, and demonstrations of rule following or socially appropriate behaviors" (Purvis, 2013, para 37).

# Recommendations for Implementing this Classroom Guidance Curriculum

## *Preparing this Classroom Guidance Curriculum*

- Guidance lesson activities are in the tier one or universal realm of multi-tiered system of supports (ASCA, 2018). This means that every child should be receiving these guidance lessons, just like every 6th grade student receives math instruction at the tier one level, for example. In addition, the entire student body should see you regularly in guidance lessons, so they know who you are and how to get to you in a crisis. Keep in mind that it is totally fine to start with baby steps–"regularly" for some school counselors might mean beginning with just one fall and one spring guidance lesson. If this is your reality, you could then work towards building in more guidance lessons each year or semester.

- The assessment activities in this curriculum include a guidance needs assessment, an informal assessment with each lesson, and an annual guidance curriculum pre/posttest to measure content knowledge gained through the curriculum. Details on how to administer the annual guidance curriculum pre/posttest as well as the informal lesson assessments are included with the first September lesson. Information on the needs assessment implementation is below.

- It is always a good idea to use data to inform your guidance curriculum content. Here are a few ways to use data to tailor this curriculum to fit the exact needs of your school and student population.
  - **Needs Assessment–**Send out the needs assessment survey (attached as a September lesson reproducible) to teachers, parents, and staff with the topics of this guidance curriculum, asking them if they feel any additional topics should be added. Google forms, website newsletters, guidance lesson announcements, and staff emails are all effective mediums to gather your needs assessment data.

  - **School Data Reports–** Review school data reports related to issues such as discipline referrals, absences, and failing grades to determine what school success or positive coping habits (PCH) topics should be emphasized or repeated (ASCA, 2016). For example, one year my colleagues and I noticed that the greatest number of discipline referrals came from students fighting so we infused every guidance lesson with an additional PCH in the form of a 5-10 minute conflict resolution review and role play. Analyze your end-of-year data in these same school data report areas to pinpoint where your guidance lessons had a positive impact on student data (ASCA, 2016). Share whatever successes you notice with your campus stakeholders (principal, staff, etc.) to encourage their continued or additional support for guidance lessons.

- There are many different ways that you can schedule your lessons. Here are a few steps that I have used myself with success:
  > First present your guidance curriculum plan to your principal or administrator to get their buy-in and to incorporate their ideas into your guidance plan. Make sure you have approval for the when/where of your guidance lessons; mentioning this approval can be a great help in scheduling lessons with reluctant teachers.

  > Next, make face-to-face contact with the teachers of the classes you will be teaching guidance lessons to. Just spend a few minutes introducing yourself and your program (if necessary) and letting them know what the guidance curriculum will entail.

  > Send teachers a follow up email with the guidance lesson topics and some proposed dates. See my example below:

Hello Ms. Frizzle,
Thanks so much for allowing me to work with students in your classrooms! On the 3rd Wednesday of the month, I'll pop in during each of your class periods for a 60 minute guidance lesson. Our lesson will cover the following general topics:

- Reminding students about how to get help from the counseling office
- Giving students information about positive coping habits and school success strategies
- Answering any student questions

I will send you a detailed lesson plan one week before the lesson is scheduled.

If any of the third Wednesdays occur during testing or holidays, I'll meet with you that week about when we can reschedule.

Let me know if this doesn't work for you. Thanks!
Ms. Lerner

**Admin Team, you are on this email so you know when/where the guidance lessons will occur. Feel free to join us anytime!*

- There are many different ways that you can plan the logistics of your lessons. Here are a few effective options that work well.
  > If you have a counseling classroom, have teachers bring their classes to your room. That way, students will know where you are and you will have all your materials at your fingertips.

  > If you have only a small office and there is an advisory or homeroom class at your school, make a rotating plan to visit each classroom during their advisory/homeroom to teach your lesson. Alternately, you can do the same with a class elective or core subject- just make sure every student on campus takes that class so they will experience your guidance lesson rotation; for example, at my school we did our lesson rotations through science in non-tested grades, and through the tech classes in the older grades. It also really helped to have everyone at a computer when we went in to do guidance lessons. Remember that mentioning principal buy-in can be a great help in scheduling your lessons with reluctant teachers (who, of course, will be won over once they actually witness your amazing lessons and the helpful effects they have on student success).

  > Alternately, if it works for your schedule, send a guidance lesson time slot signup sheet around to your staff at the beginning of each semester and let teachers choose the weekly or monthly lesson time that works best for them. This is a very popular model at the elementary level.

- Give parents/community a snapshot or summary of your guidance curriculum topics. You can do this through parent presentations at school events such as Back to School Night, or post the topics for each lesson on your counselor website or newsletter. Here is an example:

> **FEBRUARY GUIDANCE NEWSLETTER**
> **Topic, Resources, & How Parents Can Help**
>
> Hello Parents and Families!
> In February, as we come upon state testing season, we will be learning about how to healthfully manage our stress and anger. We will also continue to practice conflict resolution, safety skills, and school success strategies, as we do in every guidance lesson. Counselors will discuss how students can identify and manage their stress and anger. We will also discuss how we can support students with academic or social-emotional issues. One of the main ways parents can support their children during testing season is encourage and model positive coping habits. A positive coping habit is something healthful that a person does if they are feeling stressed or angry, for example taking a walk, talking to a friend, or writing about it in a journal. You can visit the Resources Page of this website for some resources that parents can use to support their children and reinforce our February guidance topics.
>
> Sincerely,
> Your School Counselors

## *Teaching this Classroom Guidance Curriculum*

- Teach these lessons to an entire class of students in their classroom with the teacher present. Each month's lesson plan includes one hour of activities to accomplish the objectives, which can be taught in a monthly lesson, broken into two 30-minute lessons, or even taught weekly in 20-minute segments with some additional activities added in.

- Guidance lessons always work better with teacher buy-in. The best way to get this buy-in is to communicate the guidance lesson topics you are teaching that month and to also elicit teacher feedback on what guidance topics they'd like you to cover. It is also important to ask staff what student concerns they have and discuss how you might address these in guidance lessons (i.e., you might do this through attending weekly or monthly teacher planning meetings). Make sure the teacher stays in the room while you teach your guidance lesson. This is important for building up teachers/staff as team members supporting student wellness as well as keeping you out of the disciplinarian role. That being said, classroom management is an important part of your guidance or counseling lessons. A few guidance classroom management tips to remember are:
  - You have great power to set the emotional tone- if you are excited, they will be excited.
  - Wait until you have everyone's attention before you address the class to give directions or instruction.
  - Follow these steps to give directions: say one direction at a time, then point to the direction in writing, then randomly select a student to repeat the direction to the class. Limit directions to just 3 or less at a time.

- Each lesson ends with discussion questions. The questions are provided as additional opportunities to process or lengthen the lesson, as needed.

- If you would like to learn more about any of the strategies or activities in this guidance curriculum, please refer to the professional sources listed in the references at the end.

# American School Counselor Association
# STANDARDS ALIGNMENT

The American School Counselor Association (ASCA) sets the national framework for a model school counseling program. As a result, the Overcoming Strife in Life lessons are aligned with the following ASCA Mindsets & Behaviors that can be applied to the domains of Academic, Career, and Personal/Social Development.

**MINDSETS**

| | |
|---|---|
| M 1. | Belief in development of whole self, including a healthy balance of mental, social/emotional and physical well-being |
| M 2. | Self-confidence in ability to succeed |
| M 3. | Sense of belonging in the school environment |
| M 6. | Positive attitude toward work and learning |

**BEHAVIORS**

| | |
|---|---|
| B-SS 1. | Use effective oral and written communication skills and listening skills |
| B-LS 2. | Demonstrate creativity |
| B-SMS 2. | Demonstrate self-discipline and self-control |
| B-SS 2. | Create positive and supportive relationships with other students |
| B-LS 3. | Use time-management, organizational and study skills |
| B-SS 3. | Create relationships with adults that support success |
| B-SS 4. | Demonstrate empathy |
| B-LS 5. | Apply media and technology skills |
| B-SMS 5. | Demonstrate perseverance to achieve long- and short-term goals |
| B-SS 5. | Demonstrate ethical decision making and social responsibility |
| B-SMS 6. | Demonstrate ability to overcome barriers to learning |
| B-SS 6. | Use effective collaboration and cooperation skills |
| B-LS 7. | Identify long- and short-term academic, career and social/emotional goals |
| B-SMS 7. | Demonstrate effective coping skills when faced with a problem |
| B-SS 8. | Demonstrate advocacy skills and ability to assert self, when necessary |
| B-SMS 9. | Demonstrate personal safety skills |
| B-SMS 10. | Demonstrate ability to manage transitions and ability to adapt to changing situations and responsibilities |

(ASCA, 2019, p.3)

# SEPT. LESSON Introductions & Key Guidance Concepts

**TOPIC OVERVIEW**

**The student will:**

- Begin building a relationship with the counselor and learn the counselor's role in the school
- Explore crisis prevention and how the counselor can help with crises
- Differentiate between crises and non-crises
- Identify the meaning of a positive coping habit
- Start establishing strategies for continued success in school

**Materials**

- Reproducibles (attached at the end of this session):
  - > Guidance Curriculum Needs Assessment
  - > Annual Guidance Curriculum Pre/Posttest
  - > Introductory Ice Breaker Activity
  - > Crisis Prevention Activity
  - > What is a Crisis?
  - > Counselor Request Forms
  - > Crisis vs Non-Crisis Cards
  - > What is School Success?
- Pencils
- Chart paper
- Markers
- Note cards

**Procedures**

**This initial guidance lesson runs a bit long at 75 minutes. Feel free to break it into 2 different class visits or cut out some of the activities to save time.*

1. Introduction with Scaling (10 minutes): Welcome the students to this first guidance lesson by telling them your name and a brief summary of what you will be doing with them today in this first lesson. Discuss what scaling is with the class (i.e., scaling is a way to use numbers to show how we are feeling and how our day or week is going). Ask students to think about how they are feeling right now. Have them hold up their fingers to show the number that represents this. If time, ask for a few students to explain why they have chosen their particular scaling number and/or what would make their number go up one point higher on the scale.

2. Pretest (5 minutes): Have students complete the attached pretest by guiding them through the instructions on the Annual Guidance Curriculum Pre/Posttest. Alternately, if your class is in session in August, you can complete this pretest at that time, along with one of the Additional Activities at the end of this guide. Collect and keep the pretest for data analysis purposes (see the attached Annual Guidance Curriculum Pre/Posttest counselor instructions for data guidance).

3. Ice Breaker Activity (15 minutes): Begin with a short ice breaker to introduce yourself to the class. Use the attached Introductory Ice Breaker Activity with the class to guide them through using a headline to introduce themselves and explore the role of the school counselor (use the American School Counselor Association's "Appropriate and Inappropriate Activities for School Counselors" if you need guidance on the appropriate school counselor role; you can find this document at https://www.schoolcounselor.org/asca/media/asca/home/appropriate-activities-of-school-counselors.pdf). Make sure to model the two types of headlines first as an example so everyone understands. **If your students are very young or you are pressed for time, you can have them just say their 2 headlines, rather than writing them on the reproducible. Then tell the class if that headline is part of your counselor role or not.*

# Introductions & Key Guidance Concepts

**Procedures** *(continued)*

4. Positive Coping Habit–Dealing with Crises (15 minutes): Ask the class what they think a positive coping habit is (a habit or activity that leads them feel better when they are upset or feeling negative about something in their life). Discuss that in every guidance lesson, the class will learn a new positive coping habit (PCH) and that today's PCH is how to safely handle a crisis. Lead the students through the steps on the attached Crisis Prevention Activity.

5. School Success Strategy–Exploring School Success (15 minutes): Have students work together to explore the main elements of school success. Begin by writing "School Success Strategies" at the top of a piece of chart paper and then have students give ideas on various strategies to be successful in school. Use the steps in the What is School Success? reproducible on page __to facilitate this exploration.

6. Wrap Up (10 minutes): Briefly review with the class that today they discussed crisis prevention and school success; guide them to the idea that these two topics are closely linked since preventing crisis helps us to be successful in school because we aren't spending time out of class on a crisis. Give students a note card and instruct them to write down one important thing they learned about success in school and one important thing they learned about handling a crisis. Collect the note cards for use in next month's guidance lesson.

7. Informal Assessment (5 minutes): Have students show a thumbs up or thumbs down as you read them each of the following lesson assessment statements:

   - I understood this lesson.
   - I enjoyed this lesson.
   - I know how to get immediate help for a "3 Hurts" crisis.
   - I know the meaning of "school success."
   - My scaling number has increased from the one I showed at the beginning of the class.

   **Take note of any thumbs down responses- consider meeting individually with a student who gave a thumbs down to discuss or teach further; alternately if there are many students showing thumbs down for a certain statement, consider reteaching that concept or revising your future lesson activities to include different types of activities that the students will enjoy more.*

**Discussion Questions**

- What was the most important thing you learned today about how to handle a crisis?
- What are some examples of crisis prevention that we learned?
- Why it is important to know how to prevent crisis?
- If your scaling number went up from the beginning of class to the end, how did this happen? What made your number increase? What would make it increase even higher?

# Guidance Curriculum Needs Assessment

*Counselor Instructions & Information*

Guidance curriculum needs assessments are an absolute necessity for planning a yearly guidance curriculum. Send the following needs assessment below to parents, teachers, and staff at the beginning of the school year (alternately, if you want to get a head start on guidance planning, you can send it out at the end of the previous school year). Feel free to print it out and use as is or turn it into a Google Form, Survey Monkey, or any other medium of your choice. The results will show what you can remove or add to this guidance curriculum, based on adult perceptions of student needs.
***You can also use this same resource as a student needs assessment by changing the word "student" to "I" and pre-teaching key vocabulary that students may not know.*

## Needs Assessment

Dear Parents and Staff,
Here are some topics that we might explore in future guidance lessons. Please put a check under the YES column if you think students need to learn about the topic or a check in the NO column if you don't think students need to learn about the topic.

Thank you, Your School Counselor

| GUIDANCE TOPIC | **YES** Students need info on this topic. | **NO** Students don't need info on this topic. |
|---|---|---|
| How to Get Help for Crisis/Emergency | | |
| How to Meet with Counselor for Non-Crisis Issues | | |
| Coping Skills | | |
| Conflict Resolution | | |
| Importance of Gratitude & Hope | | |
| Friendship Skills | | |
| Supporting Others in Need | | |
| Mental Health Information | | |
| Stress Management | | |
| Anger Management | | |
| Growth Mindset | | |
| Non-Verbal Communication Skills | | |
| Child Abuse Prevention | | |
| Benefits of College | | |
| Types of Careers | | |
| College Preparation Steps | | |
| Financial Aid for College | | |
| Study Skills | | |
| School Materials Organization | | |
| How to Use/Organize Your Notebook | | |
| How to Check/Improve Your Grades | | |
| Bullying Prevention | | |

*What other topics do you think students need to learn about, if any?*

# Annual Guidance Curriculum Pre/Posttest

*Counselor Instructions & Information*

Separate these counselor instructions from the Student Pretest below and have the students complete the attached pretest, either electronically (such as through Google Forms) or in a paper-based form. Administer the pretest in your first guidance lesson of the school year by reading each question aloud to the class as students independently mark their response to the question. Collect the pretests and analyze the pretest data. Then save these completed pretests until the last guidance lesson when you will use them again to be completed as the guidance curriculum posttest. At that point you will be able to compile the posttest data; then compare the data from both the pretest and posttest to share those findings with your admin team in order to advocate and plan for your counseling program. ***If you are using these resources with younger students, consider trimming it down by half and removing the statements that may not apply to your age group.*

## Student Pre/Posttest

Below are some statements for you to answer about our counseling program. Please answer each question honestly by writing your answer in the correct column.

| PRETEST | STATEMENTS | POSTTEST |
|---|---|---|
| ❑ YES<br>❑ NO<br>❑ I DON'T KNOW | Do you know your counselor's name and office location? | ❑ YES<br>❑ NO<br>❑ I DON'T KNOW |
| ❑ YES<br>❑ NO<br>❑ I DON'T KNOW | Do you know the different ways that your counselor can help students at school? | ❑ YES<br>❑ NO<br>❑ I DON'T KNOW |
| ❑ YES<br>❑ NO<br>❑ I DON'T KNOW | If you have a crisis, do you know how get help right away? | ❑ YES<br>❑ NO<br>❑ I DON'T KNOW |
| ❑ YES<br>❑ NO<br>❑ I DON'T KNOW | Do you know how to request to talk to your counselor for a non-crisis issue? | ❑ YES<br>❑ NO<br>❑ I DON'T KNOW |
| ❑ YES<br>❑ NO<br>❑ I DON'T KNOW | Can you state at least three strategies for improving your grades in school? | ❑ YES<br>❑ NO<br>❑ I DON'T KNOW |
| ❑ YES<br>❑ NO<br>❑ I DON'T KNOW | Can you state at least three positive coping habits for feeling better if you are having a bad day or having a bad memory? | ❑ YES<br>❑ NO<br>❑ I DON'T KNOW |

# Introductory Ice Breaker Activity

*Student Reproducible*

This activity is an ice breaker, which means it will help us all get to know each other better. Listen carefully as the counselor reads you a few headlines from this week's news. You will have to create your own headline in a moment, so pay attention to what a headline sounds like as you hear it. Next, everyone in the class will introduce themselves by creating one headline describing themselves and then a second headline describing the job they think the counselor does. Let's read over and follow the directions below to "break the ice" together!

***Directions:***

1. Listen to the news headlines the counselor reads to the class.
2. Write your own two headlines on the card below. Your first headline should summarize who you are (for example: 9th grade student loves to eat pizza and earn A's in math!!) The second headline should be about what you think school counselors do in their job role (for example: School Counselor rushes to work every day to help students solve their most upsetting problems!)
3. Once you write your headlines below, give this paper to the counselor who will read some or all of the headlines. As the headlines are read aloud, the class will have a chance to guess which student the first headline is referring to. Then everyone will show a thumbs up or down if the second headline correctly explains the job of the school counselor or not.
4. After the headline sharing, the counselor will discuss a bit more about their job role and the three major ways that they support students–through weekly or monthly guidance lessons, though counseling groups, and though individual sessions for requests and crises.

## Headline One *(About You)*

______________________________

______________________________

______________________________

______________________________

## Headline Two *(About the Job Duties of the School Counselor)*

______________________________

______________________________

______________________________

______________________________

# Crisis Prevention Activity

*Counselor Instructions & Information*

Dealing with student crises is one of the counselor's most important jobs. Likewise, incorporating a crisis prevention strategy as a positive coping habit into every guidance lesson is an effective way to increase student safety. Use the following crisis resources to guide your students through an introduction to crisis prevention. Show the class the following crisis information and discuss each point. Then hand out a crisis vs non-crisis slip to each student/pair and have them put it in the correct category on the board.

## CRISIS POINTS

- Teach the class what defines a crisis by showing the following What is a Crisis? information.
- Have students brainstorm different situations that could fall into each of the "3 Hurts" categories.
- Tell students that they should tell you or another adult immediately if they have a crisis.
- Be sure to let students know that all adults in the school building must enlist the help of another adult (counselor, principal, nurse, parent, CPS, etc.) in a crisis to help keep the student safe.
- Discuss with students the procedure for how to request to talk with the counselor about a non-crisis issue. Ask students what kinds of non-crisis topics they might come to see the counselor about.

## REQUESTS TO SEE THE COUNSELOR

It is crucial to tell students the protocol for how they can access you and request an appointment with you. I start off all guidance lessons with a reminder to students of how I can support them. During this reminder, I make sure they understand that they must request an appointment with me through request forms (for non-emergencies). A paper-based request form template is provided following this explanation. However, if your students are very young or if you are a paperless campus, you may want to use teacher referrals instead.

Alternately, for students that need to talk in a virtual school counseling setting, it may be best to have them email or fill out a Google form–it's easy to set up and you can find a tutorial at this URL:
**https://www.google.com/forms/about/**

Provide an intro and instructions with your google form, an example is provided below. You can also video yourself telling students this italicized info below as well as posting it on your website and the homepage of your online platform. See the Way to Goal recommendation section if you need guidance on how to meet with an individual student virtually.

*Students should email their counselor if they need help with a counseling issue. You can also "meet" with me by signing up for a time below. I'll send you an invite with the time we will meet in Google hangouts. You'll need to have your Google Hangout app downloaded to your phone/device to be able to use it so we can "meet." Remember the "3 Hurts"! If there is a concern that you may harm yourself or others, or that someone is causing you harm, I will notify the appropriate persons. Also, confidentiality cannot be guaranteed in virtual meetings due to the nature of the "cloud."*

# What is a Crisis?

*Student Reproducible*

**A CRISIS IS ONE OF THE 3 PHYSICAL HURTS:**

## Someone hurts or threatens you.

## You hurt or want to hurt another person.

## You hurt or think of hurting yourself.

***If you have a 3 hurts crisis, tell the counselor or a trusted adult IMMEDIATELY!***

# Counselor Request Form

*Student Reproducible*

## COUNSELOR REQUEST FORM

Name ______________________________ Grade ____ Date __________

*I NEED TO SEE THE COUNSELOR:*

❑ **Right away!**

❑ **As soon as possible.**

❑ **When she/he has time. I'm in no rush.**

## COUNSELOR REQUEST FORM

Name ______________________________ Grade ____ Date __________

*I NEED TO SEE THE COUNSELOR:*

❑ **Right away**

❑ **As soon as possible**

❑ **When she/he has time. I'm in no rush.**

# Crisis vs. Non-Crisis Slips

*Counselor Instructions & Information*

Cut out each of the following slips and distribute one slip to each student or pair with a little piece of tape. Write a T chart on the whiteboard or chart paper, with crisis listed as one column and non-crisis listed as the other column. Allow students to tape up their slip in the proper category on the T chart. Finally, read aloud the slips in each category of the T chart- have the students show a thumb up or down if they feel it is in the proper category. After this activity, ask the class how/why they think a knowing how to handle a crisis is a PCH.

**If you work with very young students, you might want to remove some of the more mature scenarios below.*

| | |
|---|---|
| A girl is bleeding in the bathroom, saying that she cut herself on purpose. | Two boys are yelling at each other and threatening to fight. |
| A fourth-grade student is very sad because no one will play with him at recess. | A seventh-grade student just told you that if she hears one more rumor, she is going to fight the kids who are spreading the rumors. |
| Your friend has bruises on her legs and she said she got beat up by a family member last night. | A fifth-grade student is furious that they failed their state reading test for the third time. |
| You got an A on your science test and you must tell someone! | A tenth-grade student's mom gave her a new puppy for her birthday and she can't wait to show pictures of the puppy to her counselor. |
| You don't have any proof, but you think there will be a fight after school. | A student says a teacher shoved her, but no one believes that it is true. |
| One of the seniors just broke up with her boyfriend and she is sad and withdrawn. | Joao, a sixth-grader, says that there is no food in his house because his parents went on a trip last week and he is living by himself now. |
| You are afraid to go home after school because you failed your math test and your stepdad might hit you as a consequence. | You don't like school anymore since kids started making fun on your new purple hair color, calling you Grimace. |
| A middle schooler is feeling heartbroken that they didn't make the cheer team. | Every day you see a junior name-calling the same freshman student. |

# What is School Success?

### *Counselor Instructions & Information*

Success in school is a protective factor for students experiencing trauma (CDC, 2009), so improving grades is an important trauma-informed strategy. You can work this protective factor into each of your guidance lessons by teaching a 10 minute "Getting Great Grades" strategy on various organizational, academic, or study skills strategies. Follow the steps below to introduce school success strategies to your students with this What is School Success? activity.

1. Begin by writing "School Success Strategies" at the top of a piece of chart paper. Write the following four strategies on the chart paper and discuss that students experience success in school when they:

   > Do their best work in each class.

   > Turn in all assignments.

   > Attend school daily and follow the school rules.

   > Ask for help when they need it.

2. Have students use the Turn-and-Talk technique* to brainstorm other strategies to be successful in school.
3. Write their ideas on the same piece of chart paper so you can display and use these ideas in future lessons. Spend some time discussing each of their ideas that you write on the chart paper, especially the first four strategies above.
4. Let the class know that they will be learning specific ways to implement these strategies in future guidance lessons.

**Turn-and-Talk: This is a cooperative learning technique where students brainstorm ideas on a given topic for a few minutes with a student or two sitting nearby. Usually after the Turn-and-Talk period is over, the pairs or trios will participant in a whole class share-out of the ideas they generated in their groupings.*

OCT. LESSON

# Let's Resolve Some Conflicts!

## TOPIC OVERVIEW

**The student will:**

- Review the difference between crises and non-crises
- Identify and practice the Four Steps in Conflict Resolution as a positive coping habit
- Apply the main strategies for academic success through a bingo game

**Materials**

- Reproducibles (attached at the end of this session):
  - > Conflict Resolution & Antibullying Activity
  - > Four Steps in Conflict Resolution
  - > School Success Bingo
- Pencils
- Completed wrap up note cards (from the last lesson)
- Bingo chips
- "School Success Strategies" (student-generated chart list from last lesson)
- The New York Spectrum News article titled, "By Her Own Design: A Bullied Teen Turned Fashion Designer" by Shannan Ferry Manhattan. You can find it at this URL: **https://www.ny1.com/nyc/all-boroughs/news/2020/02/22/by-her-own-design--a-bullied-teen-turned-fashion-designer** (Alternately, if you don't want to use this article, you can use any book or article with a bullying theme.)

**Procedures**

1. Introduction (10 minutes): Begin the guidance lesson by reintroducing yourself and your role to students. Then use the wrap up note cards collected from the last guidance lesson to foster a brief review of the crisis information provided in the last lesson. Facilitate this review by reading several note card crisis statements to the class. Have the class show a thumbs up/down if they feel the statement is accurate or not; as you read the statements, make sure to review the main points students need to know about handling crises vs non-crises in order to keep everyone safe:

   > The "3 Hurts Crisis" and how to get immediate help for it

   > The procedures for how to see the counselor for non-crises

   > The limits of confidentiality (i.e.,: the "3 Hurts" cannot be kept secret)

2. Scaling (5 minutes): Lead students in the following brief scaling activity. Ask students to think about how they are feeling right now. Have them hold up their fingers to show the number that represents this. If time, ask for a few students to explain why they have chosen their particular scaling number and/or what would make their number go up one point higher on the scale.

3. Positive Coping Habit–Conflict Resolution & Anti-Bullying (15 minutes): Review the meaning of a positive coping habit, or PCH, from the last lesson (a habit or activity that leads them feel better when they are feeling upset/negative about something in their life). Discuss that today's PCH will be about how to resolve conflict and handle bullying situations. Lead the students through the steps on the attached Conflict Resolution & Anti-Bullying Activity.

# Let's Resolve Some Conflicts!

**Procedures** *(continued)*

4. School Success Strategy–School Success Bingo (20 minutes): Give students an opportunity to review and apply their school success strategies that they generated in the last lesson by leading them through a game of School Success Bingo. You will need to prep for this game by circling a key word in each school success strategy on the chart paper list from last lesson. For example: if one of the strategies on the list is "Organize your backpack every week," you could circle the word "backpack" so students would know that this is the strategy's key word to use on their bingo card. Then the students will write those circled key words into a random order on their bingo card.
   **Alternately, if you are short on time or if your students are very young, give them preprinted bingo cards. You can further simplify the game for young students by giving them bingo boards that are already filled in with only 5 school success strategies.*

5. Wrap Up (5 minutes): Have students tell a partner how the Four Steps in Conflict Resolution could help someone to avoid or prevent a "3 Hurts Crisis." Share out ideas with the class.

6. Informal Assessment (5 minutes): Have students show a thumbs up or thumbs down as you read them each of the following lesson assessment statements:

   - I understood this lesson.
   - I enjoyed this lesson.
   - I know how to use the Four Steps in Conflict Resolution to solve a problem with another person.
   - I can name 3 or more school success strategies.
   - My scaling number has increased from the one I showed at the beginning of the class.

**Take note of any thumbs down responses–consider meeting individually with a student who gave a thumbs down to discuss or teach further; alternately if there are many students showing thumbs down for a certain statement, consider reteaching that concept or revising your future lesson activities to include different types of activities that the students will enjoy more.*

**Discussion Questions**

- What was your favorite part of today's lesson? Explain why.
- How could you turn one of the strategies we used in Bingo today into a goal?
- Why would it be beneficial to have a goal about academic achievement?
- What is a "3 Hurts" crisis?

# Conflict Resolution & Antibullying Activity

*Student Reproducible*

Conflict resolution is the act of solving a problem between people. This is definitely a skill that all people need to develop, especially students! Often, bullying problems can be solved with conflict resolution. Remember that bullying is repeated (or potentially repeated), aggressive behavior that occurs between children and involves a power imbalance. Today we will practice a 4-step model in conflict resolution that will get you safely through any distressing interpersonal problem, including bullying! Read on for the steps and directions to this conflict resolution activity.

***Directions:***

1. Listen carefully as your counselor reads you "By Her Own Design, A Bullied Teen Becomes Fashion Designer", which is a true story of a student whose life was changed because of bullying. URL: **https://www.ny1.com/nyc/all-boroughs/news/2020/02/22/by-her-own-design--a-bullied-teen-turned-fashion-designer**
2. Discuss your ideas to the following questions with a partner and then in a brief class discussion:
   > How would you handle the bullying situation that student Egypt 'Ify' Ufele had to deal with in the story?
   > How is conflict resolution a positive coping habit?
3. Read and explain the Four Steps in Conflict Resolution poster with your counselor and the class.
4. Decide which of the conflict resolution steps you would you use to solve the bullying problem in the story. Show the step's number with your finger.
5. Explain why you picked this step to your partner.
6. If time, practice or observe as the counselor "bullies" a few different students in your class; each student (maybe you!) will demonstrate using the Four Steps in Conflict Resolution to solve the problem and stop the bullying.

## The 4 Steps in Conflict Resolution

1. **Ignore**
2. **Walk Away**
3. **Use an "I" message**

   *Examples:*
   - I wish you wouldn't eat my french fries at lunch.
   - I don't like it when you call me names.
4. **Tell an Adult**

# School Success Bingo

*Student Reproducible*

Everyone loves bingo, right?!? For that reason, you and your classmates will now have a chance to apply the school success strategies that you discussed in our last guidance lesson today in a bingo game!! Read on for the game directions and for how to set up your bingo board.

***Steps to Set up Your Bingo Board and Play Bingo:***

1. Your counselor will review the school success strategies from the last guidance lesson with the class. Pay careful attention to the school success strategy key words that are circled on the list because these will be the words you will focus on (and probably copy onto your bingo board).
2. Your counselor will give you a blank or filled-in bingo board. If the bingo board is blank, copy the circled school success strategy key words from the chart paper list onto your bingo board.
3. Listen carefully as the counselor calls out a bingo letter and school success strategy.
4. If you have that combination of bingo letter and strategy, raise your hand. The first student to raise their hand will be called on by the counselor to explain how that strategy leads to school success. For example, if you raise your hand because you have B-Take Notes on your bingo board, then you might say something like, "Taking notes leads to school success because if you take notes in class you will be paying more attention and learning more about the topic."
5. If you give a correct explanation, then the counselor will give you a bingo chip to put on your board. If your statement is incorrect, the counselor will not give you a bingo chip and will instead call out the next bingo letter-strategy combination.
6. The first student to get five bingo chips placed in a row, column or diagonal, calls out "BINGO" and wins a prize.
7. At the end of the game, your counselor will collect the bingo cards and chips so they can be used in future lessons.

NOV. LESSON

# The Gratitude Attitude

## TOPIC OVERVIEW

**The student will:**

- Review the difference between crises and non-crises
- Define gratitude and apply it as a mood booster and positive coping habit
- Organize their backpack as a school success strategy

**Materials**

- Reproducibles (attached at the end of this session):
  - > Creating the Gratitude Attitude!
  - > School Success Strategy: Organizing Your Backpack
- Pencils
- Note cards
- Crayons & markers
- Glue and decorative craft items, if possible
- The September lesson's student-generated chart list, titled "School Success Strategies."

**Procedures**

1. Introduction (5 minutes): Begin the guidance lesson by reintroducing yourself and your role to students. Review the main points students need to know about handling crises vs non-crises in order to keep everyone safe. Reproducibles for these are provided with the first lesson.

   > The "3 Hurts Crisis" and how to get immediate help for it

   > The procedures for how to see the counselor for non-crises

   > The limits of confidentiality (i.e., the "3 Hurts" cannot be kept secret)

2. Scaling (5 minutes): Lead students in the following brief scaling activity. Ask students to think about how they are feeling right now. Have them hold up their fingers to show the number that represents this. If time, ask for a few students to explain why they have chosen their particular scaling number and/or what would make their number go up one point higher on the scale.

3. Positive Coping Habit –Expressing Gratitude (20 minutes): Review the meaning of a positive coping habit, or PCH, from the last lesson (a habit or activity that leads them feel better when they are upset or feeling negative about something in their life). Discuss that today's PCH will be about how expressing gratitude can help improve our mood and life outlook. Lead the students through the steps on the attached Creating a Gratitude Attitude activity. It can be hard to make the connection of gratitude as a mood booster, so be sure to praise and cheerlead students throughout this activity as they start to make some of these connections.
   **If your students are not fluent readers/writers, consider pre-teaching them some of the poem vocabulary (i.e., approaches, blessings, recall, recollect) and having them draw their grateful sentence or give them a stem that they can fill in instead of having to write the entire sentence.*

# The Gratitude Attitude

**Procedures** *(continued)*

4. School Success Strategy–Organizing Your Backpack (20 minutes): Briefly review the first lesson's student-generated chart list, titled "School Success Strategies" with the class. Tell them that the first school success strategy they will practice from the list is organization of school materials. Explain that everyone will start organizing their backpacks during this lesson because they can only achieve school success when they are able to quickly locate all tools needed to learn. Use the reproducible, School Success Strategy: Organizing Your Backpack, to facilitate this activity with the students.
   ****You may want to skip the notebook organization if you work with very young children or your students are encouraged to use something other than a notebook. In that case, you could try substituting a different organizational tool (such as a system of folders) if your students/school do not use notebooks.***

5. Wrap Up (5 minutes): Have students draw a doodle of what they learned today. Collect the doodles on their way out in case you want to use them in a warmup to a future lesson.

6. Informal Assessment (5 minutes): Have students show a thumbs up or thumbs down as you read them each of the following lesson assessment statements:

   - I understood this lesson.
   - I enjoyed this lesson.
   - I know how to keep my backpack organized on a weekly basis.
   - I understand how gratitude can help someone to feel better.
   - My scaling number has increased from the one I showed at the beginning of the class.

   **Take note of any thumbs down responses- consider meeting individually with a student who gave a thumbs down to discuss or teach further; alternately if there are many students showing thumbs down for a certain statement, consider reteaching that concept or revising your future lesson activities to include different types of activities that the students will enjoy more.*

**Discussion Questions**

- How does this lesson relate to the themes of Thanksgiving?
- What is something you are looking forward to over the upcoming school break?
- How is being grateful for a school break a positive coping habit?

# Creating the Gratitude Attitude!

*Student Reproducible*

Practicing daily gratitude is a positive coping habit that we can all use! Gratitude is a feeling of thankfulness; this thankful feeling often leads to happiness and goodwill towards others. Mental health researchers believe that feeling gratitude each day can lessen negative feelings like sadness, anger, etc. (If you'd like to read some of this research, use the source at the bottom of this page). When we use gratitude as a positive coping habit to minimize negative feelings, it helps to prevent crises. Let's follow the steps below to try this out for ourselves!

## STEPS

1. Read the gratitude poem, "You've Made a Difference" together with your classmates.
2. Review the definition of gratitude from the Introduction section above and then discuss the poem's themes of gratitude with your class.
3. Complete the following activity called A Note Card from the Heart.
4. Discuss the following questions with a partner in order to process the activity.
5. Pairs can share out their responses with the class, if time.

**You've Made a Difference** *by Joanna Fuchs*

As Thanksgiving day approaches,
Our blessings we recall;
The things we are most thankful for,
We recollect them all.
You are really special,
In all you say and do.
You've made a difference in our lives;
We're thankful now for you.

*Fuchs, J. (2020). Retrieved from https://www.poemsource.com/thanksgiving-poems.html*

## A NOTE CARD FROM THE HEART

Think of someone you are grateful to have in your life- share your idea with the class if you are comfortable. The counselor will give you a note card; on the note card, write a sentence or two telling that person why you are grateful to have them in your life. Decorate the note card with some colorful drawings or crafts and think about some different ways that you could hand deliver your note or share it with your friend/family member.

## QUESTIONS TO PROCESS THE ACTIVITY

- Share your ideas on the different ways you could hand deliver your note or present it to your friend/family member.
- How could this activity help someone minimize negativity?
- How could showing gratitude be a solution to a problem?
- Why does gratitude function as a positive coping habit?
- What is it about gratitude that might help someone to prevent a crisis?

## GRATITUDE: THE RESEARCH

"Gratitude improves psychological health. Gratitude reduces a multitude of toxic emotions, from envy and resentment to frustration and regret. Robert Emmons, a leading gratitude researcher, has conducted multiple studies on the link between gratitude and well-being. His research confirms that gratitude effectively increases happiness and reduces depression" (Morin, 2015, para. 4).

Morin, A. (2015.) ***Seven scientifically proven benefits of gratitude.*** Retrieved from:https://www.psychologytoday.com/us/blog/what-mentally-strong-people-dont-do/201504/7-scientifically-proven-benefits-gratitude

# School Success Strategy: Organizing Your Backpack

*Student Reproducible*

Did you know that a well-organized backpack or school bag is your main tool for doing well in school? This lesson's school success strategy will help you to keep your main tool organized for easy and efficient use. Below are the steps to clean out and organize your backpack for optimal use.

## STEPS

1. Get a backpack organization checklist from the counselor and read it together with the class.
2. Observe how the counselor uses this checklist to organize a sample backpack.
3. Pair up with another student in order to help and get help in organizing backpacks. This student will be your "accountability partner."
4. Clean out your backpack with your "accountability partner" according to the checklist and then check off the item on the checklist; your partner's job is to check that you carefully do each item on your checklist before you check it off.
5. Make a plan with your partner for how you will clean out and organize your backpack weekly; feel free to take extra checklist sheet/s if this will help you get it done. Keep each other accountable with reminders to do the weekly backpack organization task.
6. Keep in mind that you can also fill in a request to organize your backpack (or finish today's organization) in the counselor's office.

## BACKPACK/SCHOOL BAG CHECKLIST

*Instructions:* Review each step below to organize your backpack and check off the step as you complete it for your backpack cleanout.

### *My backpack has:*

- ❑ My name written on the backpack in permanent marker
- ❑ No major rips or holes
- ❑ A workable zipper(s)
- ❑ All papers are secured in their proper binder or folder
- ❑ A notebook and homework folders with completed schoolwork inside
- ❑ 2-3 writing utensils

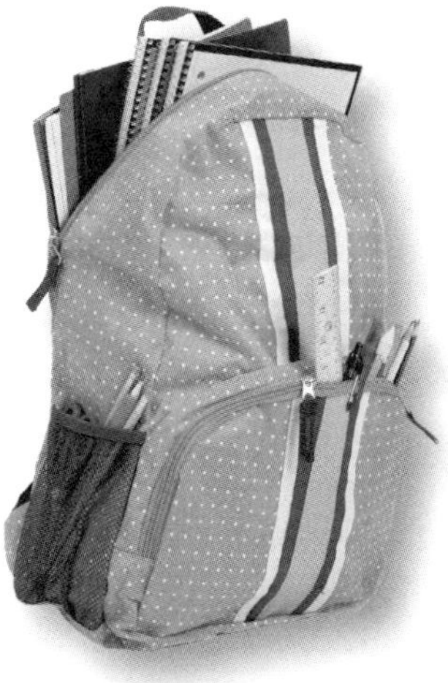

DEC. LESSON

# Be a Hope Builder

## TOPIC OVERVIEW

**The student will:**

- Review the difference between crises and non-crises
- Explore hope building through a story book experience
- Analyze how building hope in others is a positive coping habit for both the builder and the buildee
- Generate a list of how to build hope in others
- Organize their notebook as a school success strategy

**Materials**

- Reproducibles (attached at the end of this session):
  > Biblio-counseling Book List: Themes of Hope
  > School Success Strategy: Organizing Your Notebook
- *A Flicker of Hope* by Julia Cook or some other picture book with themes of hope and/or asking for help. See book list on page 107 with activity ideas.
- Pencils
- Markers and chart paper

**Procedures**

1. Introduction (5 minutes): Begin the guidance lesson by reintroducing yourself and your role to students. Review the main points students need to know about handling crises vs non-crises in order to keep everyone safe. Reproducibles for these are provided with the first lesson.

   > The "3 Hurts Crisis" and how to get immediate help for it

   > The procedures for how to see the counselor for non-crises

   > The limits of confidentiality (i.e., the "3 Hurts" cannot be kept secret)

2. Scaling (5 minutes): Lead students in the following brief scaling activity. Ask students to think about how they are feeling right now. Have them hold up their fingers to show the number that represents this. If time, ask for a few students to explain why they have chosen their particular scaling number and/or what would make their number go up one point higher on the scale.

3. Positive Coping Habit–Building Hope through Biblio-counseling (25 minutes): Review the meaning of a positive coping habit, or PCH, from the last lesson (a habit or activity that leads them feel better when they are upset or feeling negative about something in their life). Discuss that today's PCH will be about building hope; guide students to the idea that when we help others, such as through giving them hope, it naturally builds up our own feelings of self-worth. Show the picture book to the class and ask students to guess what it might be about. Read the book aloud to the class. Discuss the main theme of the story with the class as it relates to being a hope builder and how we all need hope to get through tough times. After the story, make a list with the class on chart paper of various things we can do to build hope in others if they are experiencing a difficult time (e.g., listen as they vent about their struggles, ask how you can help, play a sport with them, etc.)

4. School Success Strategy–Notebook Organization (20 minutes): Explain that everyone will start organizing their notebooks during this lesson because it is crucial to school success to have a place to keep all school papers and assignments neat and in order. Use the reproducible, School Success Strategy: Organizing Your Notebook, to facilitate this activity with the students.

# Be a Hope Builder

**Procedures** *(continued)*

5. Wrap Up (5 minutes): Have students tell a partner the most important thing they learned today. Spend a minute or two letting the class share out their partner ideas.

6. Informal Assessment (5 minutes): Have students show a thumbs up or thumbs down as you read them each of the following lesson assessment statements:

    - I understood this lesson.
    - I enjoyed this lesson.
    - I know how to keep my notebook organized on a weekly basis.
    - I understand how building hope in others can make me feel better.
    - My scaling number has increased from the one I showed at the beginning of the class.

    ***Take note of any thumbs down responses- consider meeting individually with a student who gave a thumbs down to discuss or teach further; alternately if there are many students showing thumbs down for a certain statement, consider reteaching that concept or revising your future lesson activities to include different types of activities that the students will enjoy more.**

**Discussion Questions**

- How can building hope in others be a positive coping habit?
- How can building hope in others prevent student crises?
- Why is it important to help people with a problem or with hopelessness before their problem gets to crisis mode?
- Do you think it will be hard for you to keep an organized notebook? Why or why not?

# Biblio-Counseling Book List: Themes of Hope

*Counselor Instructions & Information*

Biblio-counseling is the practice of using of books, or other media, to teach social-emotional skills, such as conflict resolution (ASCA, 2019). This form of counseling is an effective intervention to use with all ages of students! Sometimes, I meet skeptical high school counselors who don't believe this practice will work with the older kids who are transitioning into adulthood...to which I always reply that the billion-dollar audio book industry proves otherwise! Our human brains are hardwired for storytelling! Humans have evolved over millions of years of storytelling, so the sound of the human voice telling (or reading) a story is a naturally soothing and instinctual way for a person of any age to learn (Lerner, 2019).

Below are several excellent title suggestions for books that include themes of home and friendship. I've also included some ways to actively involve students during read aloud time at the bottom of this page.

## POSSIBLE READ ALOUD BOOKS:

Mommy What's Died? .......... by Linda Gill
Sunny's Time to Tell .......... by Julie Mendenhall
How Fredrick Found His Light .......... by Katherine McIntyre
Hugo Learns to Trust Again .......... by Susan Bowman
Miguel: A Deportation Story .......... by Susan Bowman
Squirmy Learns to be Mindful .......... by Joree Rose
My Daddy Is in Jail .......... by Janet Bender
Changing Young Lives One Story at a Time .......... by Tom Carr
En Mi Familia .......... by Carmen Lomas Garza
Letters to a Bullied Girl .......... by Olivia Gardner
Chicken Soup for the Teenage Soul .......... by Jack Canfield
How Are You Feelin'?, Juan Pablo Chameleon .......... by Dan St. Romain
Where the Side Walk Ends .......... by Shel Silverstein
Winnie-the-Pooh .......... by A.A. Milne
Flicker of Hope .......... by Julia Cook

### Ways to Actively Involve Students in Read Aloud Time

- Have students tell their partner what just happened in the story.
- Have a student act out the story to the class as the counselor reads aloud.
- Have pairs act out the story to each other as the counselor reads aloud.
- At the end of the read aloud time, have students close their eyes and imagine the next part of the story or its sequel. Share ideas.
- Throughout the read aloud time, have students show their thumbs- pointing up if they understand what is happening in the story, pointing down if they don't understand the story events.

# School Success Strategy: Organizing Your Notebook

*Student Reproducible*

Did you know that a well-organized notebook is another crucial tool for doing well in school? Well, it is and this lesson's school success strategy will help you learn the importance of organizing your notebook regularly. A 3-ring notebook or binder with subject-labeled section dividers will give you an orderly place to keep all your schoolwork organized by subject. Let's jump into some steps for how to do this!

**STEPS**

1. Get a notebook organization checklist from the counselor and read it together with the class.
2. Observe how the counselor uses this checklist to organize a sample notebook.
3. Pair up in order to help and get help in organizing notebooks.
4. Organize your notebook with your "accountability partner" according to the checklist and then check off the item on the checklist; your partner's job is to check that you carefully do each item on your checklist before you check it off.
5. Make a plan with your partner for how you will clean out and organize your notebook weekly; feel free to take an extra checklist sheet/s if this will help you get it done. Keep each other accountable for reminding each other to do the weekly notebook organization task!
6. Keep in mind that you can also fill in a request to organize your notebook (or finish today's organization) in the counselor's office.

## NOTEBOOK/BINDER CHECKLIST

*Instructions:* Review each step below to organize your notebook and check off the step as you complete it.

***My notebook has:***

- ❑ My name written on the front in permanent marker
- ❑ Subject sections divided with labeled tabs
- ❑ A section for each school subject
- ❑ Blank paper secured in a section(s)
- ❑ All my school work papers hole-punched and in their correct subject section
- ❑ A homework section with homework papers inside

***(Note: If using a digital organization system—work on creating folders for each subject and moving files in each subject folder)***

JAN. LESSON

# Connection Reflection

## TOPIC OVERVIEW

**The student will:**

- Review the difference between crises and non-crises
- Explore connection with others as a positive coping habit
- Make a plan for weekly grade checks in order to improve school success

**Materials**

- Reproducibles (attached at the end of this session):
  > School Success Strategy: Checking Your Grades Weekly
- Computer access and grade checking program- if students will be checking their grades online
- Pencils and paper
- The September lesson's student-generated chart list, titled "School Success Strategies."

**Procedures**

1. Introduction (5 minutes): Begin the guidance lesson by reintroducing yourself and your role to students. Review the main points students need to know about handling crises vs non-crises in order to keep everyone safe. Reproducibles for these are provided with the first lesson.

   > The "3 Hurts Crisis" and how to get immediate help for it

   > The procedures for how to see the counselor for non-crises

   > The limits of confidentiality (i.e., the "3 Hurts" cannot be kept secret)

2. Scaling (5 minutes): Lead students in the following brief scaling activity. Ask students to think about how they are feeling right now. Have them hold up their fingers to show the number that represents this. If time, ask for a few students to explain why they have chosen their particular scaling number and/or what would make their number go up one point higher on the scale.

3. Positive Coping Habit–Connecting with Other People (20 minutes): Review the meaning of a positive coping habit (PCH) as a habit or activity that leads them feel better when they are upset or feeling negative about something in their life. Discuss that today's PCH will be about making connections with others. Briefly discuss with the class that building connections and strengthening bonds between people are very important in life; as human beings, our brains are hard-wired to flourish when we interact with other people.

   Begin the activity by giving each student a paper to write 3 characteristics about themselves; no names should be written on the paper. Then, have the class circle up, crumple their papers into a ball, and throw them in the middle of the circle. Next, have each student to pick up a "snowball" that is not their own and read it aloud. Classmates should step forward if they have a similar characteristic. Finally, foster a brief discussion on the students' perceptions of: how this activity helped to build connections between classmates and how connections can improve mental health.
   **If your students struggle with writing consider having them choose and copy just one characteristic from a list that you display.*

# Connection Reflection

**Procedures** *(continued)*

5. School Success Strategy–Weekly Grades Check (20 minutes): Briefly review the first lesson's student-generated chart list, titled "School Success Strategies" with the class. Tell them that today you will teach them an academic success strategy that will help them to boost their grades! Explain that everyone will check their grades and make a plan for doing this on a weekly basis. Use the reproducible, School Success Strategy: Checking Your Grades Weekly, to facilitate this activity with the students. Tell the class that checking their grades at least once a week is one of the top strategies for academic success.
   **If you work with young children who don't have weekly grades, you might skip #4 or introduce the importance of a home study spot with them. Then, have them draw, color, and present a picture of their home study spot; if they don't have a home study spot yet, they could design their ideal one in their illustration.*

6. Wrap Up (5 minutes): Briefly review with the class that today they discussed weekly grade checks and the importance of connecting with others. Discuss the link between these two topics (i.e., if we check our grades and there is a problem, we have to "connect" with someone like a teacher/parent/counselor in order to get help to fix the problem).

7. Informal Assessment (5 minutes): Have students show a thumbs up or thumbs down as you read them each of the following lesson assessment statements:

   - I understood this lesson.
   - I enjoyed this lesson.
   - I know how to check my grades on a weekly basis.
   - I understand how connecting with others is good for my mental health.
   - My scaling number has increased from the one I showed at the beginning of the class.

   **Take note of any thumbs down responses- consider meeting individually with a student who gave a thumbs down to discuss or teach further; alternately if there are many students showing thumbs down for a certain statement, consider reteaching that concept or revising your future lesson activities to include different types of activities that the students will enjoy more.*

**Discussion Questions**

- What common characteristics did you notice that multiple students wrote on their paper snowballs?
- Connecting with other people and finding things in common is really important. Why do you think this is important?
- How do you think connection with others and/or improving your grades can help prevent a "3 Hurts" student crisis?

# School Success Strategy: Checking Your Grades Weekly

*Student Reproducible*

Succeeding academically helps you to feel good about yourself, which, in turn, boosts your mental health. Remember that school counselors are here to help if you are failing or worried about classes/grades. Today we are going to learn a school success strategy that will help you to increase your grades!

## STRATEGY #1: ELECTRONIC GRADE CHECKS

If you have access to a software or online program that tracks your grades, use it to check your grades on a weekly or daily basis. If possible, your counselor will now demonstrate the computer tutorial on how to access and review your grades and assignments. The counselor will also show you how to interpret your weekly grade averages with all the assignments listed that contribute to that average. If you don't have electronic access to your grades, or if you are just more comfortable checking your grades in a paper-based manner, read on for strategy #2.

## STRATEGY #2: PAPER GRADE CHECKS

Alternately, if your school doesn't have a computerized grade system, you can create a grade sheet by using the template below. Your counselor will explain and model how to use the attached Weekly Grade Sheet-basically, you will need to have a brief conversation with (each of) your teachers to get the information you need to fill in your Weekly Grade Sheet every Friday. After you fill in the info for the week, ask your teacher/s to initial the line of their period/subject.

**WEEKLY GRADE SHEET FOR** ______________________________ **DATE:** ______________

| PERIOD *AND/OR* SUBJECT: | GRADE AVERAGE: | COMMENTS (REASONS FOR FAILING AVERAGE, IF APPLICABLE): | TEACHER SIGNATURE: |
|---|---|---|---|
| | | | |
| | | | |
| | | | |
| | | | |
| | | | |

## MAKING A PLAN

Now, discuss with a partner how you will make a plan for checking your grades on a weekly basis. Talk through obstacles that might get in the way of your plan and how you will overcome those obstacles. Once you have talked with your partner, share you plan with the class so everyone can benefit from each other's good ideas!

FEB. LESSON

# Grow Your Mindset!

## TOPIC OVERVIEW

**The student will:**

- Review the difference between crises and non-crises
- Apply growth mindset as a positive coping habit
- Explore the benefits of college as a school success strategy

**Materials**

- Big Future's "Learn More, Earn More" infographic at URL: **https://bigfuture.collegeboard.org/get-started/know-yourself/learn-more-earn-more)**
- Video clip of Nike's Michael Jordan "Failure" commercial from **Youtube.com** *(Note: websites may change over time)*
- Internet with laptop or projector to show website infographic and online video
- Markers and chart paper
- Pencils and paper

**Procedures**

1. Introduction (5 minutes): Begin the guidance lesson by reintroducing yourself and your role to students. Review the main points students need to know about handling crises vs non-crises in order to keep everyone safe. Reproducibles for these are provided with the first lesson.

   > The "3 Hurts Crisis" and how to get immediate help for it

   > The procedures for how to see the counselor for non-crises

   > The limits of confidentiality (i.e., the "3 Hurts" cannot be kept secret)

2. Scaling (5 minutes): Lead students in the following brief scaling activity. Ask students to think about how they are feeling right now. Have them hold up their fingers to show the number that represents this. If time, ask for a few students to explain why they have chosen their particular scaling number and/or what would make their number go up one point higher on the scale.

3. Positive Coping Habit–Growth Mindset (15 minutes): Discuss that today's positive coping habit will be about using a growth mindset to have a positive and forward-moving perspective on life's challenges. Define growth mindset (the belief that people can develop their innate abilities with hard work and perseverance) with the class and show them Nike's 2006 Michael Jordan "Failure" commercial at youtube.com.

   After the commercial, process the experience with the following questions:

   - How does Michael Jordan have a growth mindset in this commercial?
   - Is failing something (like a test) the "end of the world"? Why or why not?
   - What could you learn from a failure? (retake the test, do test corrections, etc.)
   - How does having a growth mindset function as a positive coping habit?
   - How could having a growth mindset help someone prevent or safely handle a student crisis?

4. School Success Habit–Learn More, Earn More (15 minutes): Show students the infographic Learn More, Earn More (you can find it at this URL: **https://bigfuture.collegeboard.org/get-started/know-yourself/learn-more-earn-more**). Guide the class in a discussion about the infographic by displaying the following questions. Explain each of the kinds of degrees listed in the infographic and the salary associated with each degree. Give students a few minutes to use the Think-Pair-Share* activity to generate some answers to the following questions:

    - Thumbs up/down if you've considered attending a university, technical/trade school or community college.

    - Have you ever talked with your parent/guardian about how much money you want to make at your future job? (Less advanced version of this question: Have you ever talked with your parent/guardian about what kind of job you want to have when you are an adult? More advanced version of this question: Have you talked with your family about how much money you might earn with the degree you need for the job you want?) If so, how did this conversation go? If not, how might you start this conversation?

    - Why do you think planning for college now is a school success strategy?

    - How will the school success strategies you are learning in guidance lessons (organizing your backpack, checking your grades weekly, etc.) help you get to college?

    *If you work with young students or if you are short on time, you can simplify this activity by decreasing the number of questions to just 2, removing the most difficult ones.*
    **Think-Pair-Share is a strategy where students first think individually about their responses to a question/prompt, then share their response with a partner, and finally share their response with the class.*

5. Wrap Up- Four Corners (10 minutes): Write the following statements, each one on a different piece of paper, and hang them in the four corners of the classroom. Have the students go to the corner with the paper that best represents how they are feeling. Once everyone is in their chosen corner, ask a few students to explain why they chose their corner. Statements:

    - In this lesson, the SCALING was most helpful to me.

    - In this lesson, LEARNING ABOUT COLLEGE was most helpful to me.

    - In this lesson, GROWTH MINDSET was most helpful to me.

    - In this lesson, REVIEWING THE "3 HURTS" was most helpful to me.

6. Informal Assessment (5 minutes): Have students show a thumbs up or thumbs down as you read them each of the following lesson assessment statements:

    - I understood this lesson.

    - I enjoyed this lesson.

    - I understand how being successful in school now can help me in college one day.

    - I understand how growth mindset is a positive coping habit.

    - My scaling number has increased from the one I showed at the beginning of the class.

    **Take note of any thumbs down responses- consider meeting individually with a student who gave a thumbs down to discuss or teach further; alternately if there are many students showing thumbs down for a certain statement, consider reteaching that concept or revising your future lesson activities to include different types of activities that the students will enjoy more.*

**Discussion Questions**

- Did you enjoy this lesson? Why or why not?

- What do you think are the most important parts of this lesson that you would teach a younger sibling or cousin?

- Who in your life does not have a growth mindset? How could you help them to develop a growth mindset?

MARCH LESSON

# Flipping Your Lid

## TOPIC OVERVIEW

**The student will:**

- Review the difference between crises and non-crises
- Learn about the stress response in the brain
- Practice 2 stress management strategies
- Analyze positive body language as a school success strategy

**Materials**

- Reproducibles (attached at the end of this session):
  > Stress Management Information & Activity
  > School Success Strategy: Body Language
- Pencils (only if you decide to have students write out some of their discussion question answers)

**Procedures**

1. Introduction (5 minutes): Begin the guidance lesson by reintroducing yourself and your role to students. Review the main points students need to know about handling crises vs non-crises in order to keep everyone safe. Reproducibles for these are provided with the first lesson.

   > The "3 Hurts Crisis" and how to get immediate help for it

   > The procedures for how to see the counselor for non-crises

   > The limits of confidentiality (i.e., the "3 Hurts" cannot be kept secret)

2. Scaling (5 minutes): Lead students in the following brief scaling activity. Ask students to think about how they are feeling right now. Have them hold up their fingers to show the number that represents this. If time, ask for a few students to explain why they have chosen their particular scaling number and/or what would make their number go up one point higher on the scale.

3. Positive Coping Habit–Stress Reduction (15 minutes): Ask the class how reducing stress is a positive coping habit. Tell them you will be giving them information and teaching them about calming strategies to help them when they feel stressed or worried. Lead students through the reproducible, Stress Management Information & Activity.

4. School Success Habit–Body Language (20 minutes): Ask the class if they think their body language impacts their school success (you might have to define body language for them as the non-verbal messages our body sends another person)- have them stand if they think the answer is 'yes' and sit if they think the answer is 'no'. Tell the class that in this lesson, you will show them the impact that their classroom body language has on their school success. Use the reproducible, Body Language, to guide students to this understanding.

5. Wrap Up (5 minutes): Have students tell a partner the most important thing they learned today. Spend a minute or two letting the class share out their partner ideas.

6. Informal Assessment (5 minutes): Have students show a thumbs up or thumbs down as you read them each of the following lesson assessment statements:

    - I understood this lesson.
    - I enjoyed this lesson.
    - I know how body language influences my success in school.
    - I know at least 2 stress reduction strategies to calm my fear or anger.
    - My scaling number has increased from the one I showed at the beginning of the class.

    **Take note of any thumbs down responses–consider meeting individually with a student who gave a thumbs down to discuss or teach further; alternately if there are many students showing thumbs down for a certain statement, consider reteaching that concept or revising your future lesson activities to include different types of activities that the students will enjoy more.*

**Discussion Questions**

- How can positive body language lead to success in school?
- How can negative body language lead to problems in school?
- How can stress reduction strategies such as the self-hug or hand massage help prevent student crises?

# Stress Management Information & Activity

*Student Reproducible*

When people act out feeling very upset, we sometimes call it "flipping our lid". However, we have control of just how angry or stressed we let our brains get. Let's understand this further by making a hand model of the brain. As a class, let's read the following Hand Model of the Brain diagram below in order to make our own hand model of your brain.

## HAND MODEL OF THE BRAIN

**When our brain is calm and working well, it is like the closed fist below, where all parts are connected and working well together. But, when we get very stressed, angry, or afraid, our brain is like the open hand below with the different parts of the brain disconnected and not working together.**

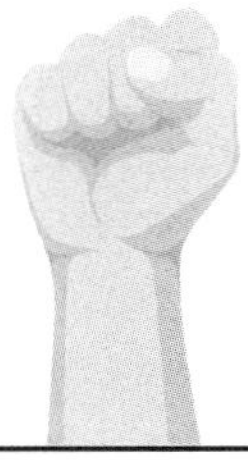

In this hand-brain model, your lower/mid brain is made up of your wrist (representing your spinal cord), your palm (representing your brain stem) and your thumb (representing your limbic region); your thumb is where your big emotions (i.e., fight or flight) live. Your upper brain is made up of your folded fingers (representing the cortex) where your higher-level thinking and learning occur– which is what you are using right now in this lesson!

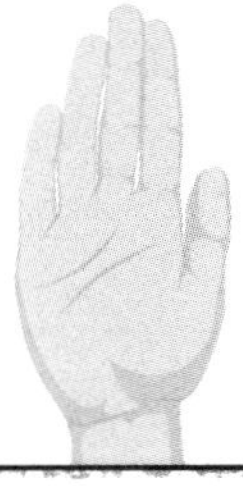

However, when you get very stressed or angry, your upper and lower brain disconnect so your brain can focus all of its energy on the mid/lower brain's fight or flight response.
When this stress response happens, it's like our fingers fly open because the upper brain is no longer connected to the lower brain; this means our upper brain is not working and thinking clearly. Some people call this "flipping your lid!"

Now let's learn two quick stress reduction strategies that you can do anywhere to help "close the lid" and calm your brain if you are feeling upset!

1. **Hand/arm self-massage:** Use your right hand to massage your left palm or arm for 10-20 seconds, then switch to your left hand massaging your right palm or arm and repeat.
2. **Self-hug:** Wrap your arms around yourself and squeeze for 10-20 seconds, then repeat 3 times. By giving ourselves contact comfort, we increase feelings of safety and reduce the nervous system's reactivity to pain and threat.

**PROCESS THE ACTIVITY:**

- By massaging our palm and/or giving a self-hug, we are triggering our parasympathetic nervous system which is our body system responsible for resting and digesting. Why do you think triggering our resting and digesting system helps us to calm down or "close the lid?"
- How are these 2 strategies positive coping habits?
- What else could you do to calm your stress and anger once you've "flipped your lid?"

# School Success Strategy: Body Language

*Student Reproducible*

Good body language in the classroom definitely impacts your success in school! Why? Because positive body language tells the teacher that you care about what is happening in the classroom; this will lead to them helping you to be successful in their class!

## BODY LANGUAGE EXPERIMENT

Let's try a body language experiment! A few volunteers will show us how they sit in their favorite and least favorite class. Next, we will give the volunteers feedback on the messages we got from the body language in how they were sitting in both their favorite and least favorite class. Watch as the counselor models this experiment first, then we'll call some volunteers to try it. Finally, we will process the experiment with the questions below and then practice in groups.

## PROCESSING THE EXPERIMENT

- What message did you get from the volunteers' positive body language and what message does this type of body language send to a teacher?

  ______________________________

  ______________________________

- What message did you get from the volunteers' negative body language and what message does this type of body language show to a teacher?

  ______________________________

  ______________________________

- Do you think positive body language is important in the classroom? Why or why not?

  ______________________________

  ______________________________

- What does positive classroom body language look like? The counselor will write your responses/actions on chart paper so we can display the positive body language list to reference if we ever need ideas.

  ______________________________

  ______________________________

## PRACTICE ACTIVITY

- In groups of 4-6 students, each student should practice an example of good body language, referring to the characteristics of good classroom body language that were just compiled on the chart paper. Group members can rate each other's body language silently by holding up fingers to show number scores on a 10 point scale.

APRIL LESSON

# Child Abuse Prevention

***Note to Counselor***

*April is National Child Abuse Prevention Month. Despite the unsettling nature of this topic, most states have laws that educators must teach students about child abuse prevention, no matter the age. Child abuse/neglect may be a difficult topic for some of your students, especially those that are experiencing family problems or changes. Nevertheless, our number one priority to children is to keep them safe. In addition, child abuse prevention education breaks the cycle of abuse. According to the American School Counselor Association, "prevention programs should focus on educating children with universal safety and prevention strategies that apply to all types of maltreatment..." (Pendarvis & Shook, 2017, p. 34). Consult with your co-counselor and/or administrator about how best to prepare students for this lesson or to address any students that get upset during the lesson. Always inform your campus administration before teaching this lesson.*

## TOPIC OVERVIEW

**The student will:**

- Review the difference between crises and non-crises
- Identify the types of child abuse
- Explore ways to practice safety and prevent child abuse
- Apply the main strategies for academic success through a bingo game

**Materials**

- Reproducibles (attached at the end of this session):
  - > Child Abuse Prevention
  - > School Success Bingo (use the completed bingo boards from the October lesson)
- Pencils
- Paper
- Crayons and markers
- Bingo chips

**Procedures**

1. Introduction (5 minutes): Begin the guidance lesson by reintroducing yourself and your role to students. Review the main points students need to know about handling crises vs non-crises in order to keep everyone safe. Reproducibles for these are provided with the first lesson.

   > The "3 Hurts Crisis" and how to get immediate help for it

   > The procedures for how to see the counselor for non-crises

   > The limits of confidentiality (i.e.,: the "3 Hurts" cannot be kept secret)

2. Scaling (5 minutes): Lead students in the following brief scaling activity. Ask students to think about how they are feeling right now. Have them hold up their fingers to show the number that represents this. If time, ask for a few students to explain why they have chosen their particular scaling number and/or what would make their number go up one point higher on the scale.

3. Positive Coping Habit–Child Abuse Prevention (25 minutes): Tell the class that today they will learn strategies on how to prevent child abuse; ask them how they feel about learning about this topic. Hand out the child abuse prevention reproducible and read through the statistics and definitions together. Give the class think time to come up with ways to get help if they or someone they know is being abused or neglected. Write their answers on chart paper. Make sure that the following suggestions, as well as the ones listed in the reproducible introduction, are included on the chart paper list:

   > Tell a trusted adult- teacher, coach, parent, counselor, school nurse, etc.

   > Call 911 and tell about the abuse/neglect.

   > Talk to a ChildHelp hotline counselor: it is free to call 1-800-4-A-CHILD (1-800-422-4453)

   > Do not be alone with anyone who hurts you.

   After the chart paper list is done, brainstorm with the class some ways they could share this info with other kids. **If you work with teen students, make sure they understand that teen dating violence (TDV) is considered child abuse. Foster a brief discussion about TDV- how to prevent it (same strategies on chart paper above) and how students feel talking about it. If needed, you can find information on TDV in the Centers for Disease Control and Prevention's article "Preventing Teen Dating Violence" at URL:* ***https://www.cdc.gov/violenceprevention/intimatepartnerviolence/teendatingviolence/fastfact.html*** *(Note that websites change over time).*

4. School Success Habit–School Success Bingo (15 minutes): Since the child abuse prevention activity for this lesson is so intense and can run long, let students have a break with a simple and fun school success bingo game. You can use the same bingo steps and bingo boards from the October lesson.

5. Wrap Up (5 minutes): Have students do a 5 minute free write (or free draw if they are very young or struggle with writing) on how they would teach other kids about the child abuse prevention strategies that they learned. Choose a few students to share their responses with the class.

6. Informal Assessment (5 minutes): Have students show a thumbs up or thumbs down as you read them each of the following lesson assessment statements:

   - I understood this lesson.
   - I know some strategies for keeping myself and others safe from child abuse/neglect.
   - My scaling number has increased from the one I showed at the beginning of the class.

   **Take note of any thumbs down responses- consider meeting individually with a student who gave a thumbs down to discuss or teach further; alternately if there are many students showing thumbs down for a certain statement, consider reteaching that concept or revising your future lesson activities to include different types of activities that the students will enjoy more.*

**Discussion Questions**

- What was the most challenging part of participating in this lesson?
- How do you think learning about child abuse can help prevent student crises?
- What messages are important to share with all students about this topic?
- What is your favorite school success strategy? Why?

# Child Abuse Prevention

*Student Reproducible*

Child abuse is a tough subject to talk about, but it is important for kids to know how to keep themselves safe! For that reason, you will be learning about the different types of child abuse today and how to prevent them. Every student needs to know that: no one has the right to abuse anyone, no one deserves to be abused, and it is never the victim's fault. Always listen to your inner voice if it tells you that something happening to you isn't right. Let's start with some statistics that show us just how important this topic is!

## CHILD ABUSE STATISTICS

- Children from all religions, ethnic groups, and cultures are affected by child abuse.
- Child abuse affects 700,000 children in the US each year.
- Child Protective Services helps more than 3 million children each year.

*(Source: Retrieved from https://americanspcc.org/child-abuse-statistics/)*

## CHILD ABUSE VOCABULARY

- **Physical Abuse**
  A physical injury or threat of a physical injury that causes serious harm to the child (such as punching, beating, shaking, kicking, hitting, burning, etc.)

- **Neglect**
  Neglect occurs when a parent or caregiver does not take care of their child's basic needs, such as healthcare, food, shelter, and clothing (this excludes failure caused by financial inability unless services have been offered and refused by parent/caregiver).

- **Sexual Abuse**
  Sexual abuse includes harming a child by: touching any of the areas a bathing suit covers, involving them in indecent exposure, or exposing them to pornographic materials.

- **Emotional Abuse**
  Emotional abuse causes mental or emotional injury that impairs the child's growth, development, or psychological functioning.

## HELPING OTHERS

What are some ways to get help if you or someone you know is being abused or neglected? How could we share information about ways to get help with other students?

______________________________________________

______________________________________________

MAY LESSON

# Wishes for the Future

## TOPIC OVERVIEW

**The student will:**

- Review the difference between crises and non-crises
- Experience hope for the future by reading and illustrating a story about wishes
- Review main topics learned this year
- Complete a guidance posttest to show knowledge gained this year from guidance curriculum

**Materials**

- Reproducible:
  > Guidance Curriculum Annual Pre/Posttest (same version that was half-completed by students in the September lesson)
- "The Silver Fish" from *Where the Sidewalk Ends* by Shel Silverstein OR *Winnie-the-Pooh* by A. A. Milne (passage about Pooh receiving gift and leaving with Piglet- located in the last 3-5 pages of book). Alternately, you can use a different story of your choice with themes of hope/wishes for the future.
- Pencils
- Paper
- Crayons and markers

**Procedures**

1. Introduction (5 minutes): Begin the guidance lesson by reintroducing yourself and your role to students. Review the main points that students need to know about handling crises vs non-crises in order to keep everyone safe. Reproducibles for these are provided with the first lesson. Explain to students that this will be the last guidance lesson of the school year since summer break is coming soon.

2. Scaling (5 minutes): Lead students in the following brief scaling activity. Ask students to think about how they are feeling about school ending for the year. Have them scale their feelings using fingers.

3. Positive Coping Habit–Wishes for the Future (20 minutes): Tell students that people reflect on their wishes and hopes at the end of the school year since it is a time of endings and new beginnings. Ask the class how this reflection could function as a positive coping habit (focusing on hopes for the future lifting us up rather than getting bogged down with the negative feelings that something is ending). Explain that for this last guidance lesson, the class will read a poem or story passage together to explore the themes of wishes, endings, and new beginnings. Read the "Silver Fish" poem or the last few pages of Winnie-the-Pooh aloud to the class; even though these are parts of picture books, their themes and vocabulary make them appropriate for secondary students as well as elementary students. Once you have finished reading, briefly discuss the themes of wishes, endings, and/or new beginnings. Next, ask students what their wishes are for the summer. Give the students blank paper and have them draw and color their wish for the summer.

4. School Success Strategy–Review and Posttest (20 minutes): Tell the class that in this final guidance lesson, they will have a chance to reflect on all the school success strategies that they have learned this year. Give the class a minute of think time to reflect on the main points (both school success and positive coping habits, as well as crisis info) that they learned in guidance lessons this year. Write their ideas on chart paper; at this point, students should be able to cover all topics listed on the posttest. Next, distribute or access the same Guidance Curriculum Annual Pre/Posttest from the September lesson that students completed- now they will complete the posttest section of this same assessment. Read the posttest aloud and have the students complete it.

MAY LESSON

# Wishes for the Future

**Procedures** *(continued)*

5. After the posttests are collected or closed out, have students tell a partner which school success strategy they think will help them the most in their future. Share out their responses and then foster a brief discussion of the best way to keep practicing their top success strategies, even though guidance lessons are ending.
   ***After the lesson, compare the data from both the pretest and posttest to share those findings with your admin team in order to advocate and plan for your counseling program.***

6. Wrap Up (10 minutes): Wrap up the lesson by allowing students to do a Gallery Walk to view each other's wishes for their summer/future.

**Discussion Questions**

- How are you feeling about the guidance lessons ending for the school year?
- What do you feel was your greatest success this school year?
- What could you do in the future to have more of this success during the next school year?

# Additional Activities

*Counselor Instructions & Information*

As mentioned in the recommendations section, these are additional activities for extending your curriculum. These activities have been created to extend this guidance curriculum past the nine lessons that are provided in this book. In addition, these activities can be added into existing lessons if you'd like to extend their length past one hour. You can also substitute any of the additional activities for a particular lesson activity if that particular one won't work with your students.

## Free Writing

Give the class 10-15 minutes to free write on any topic that is causing them to feel strongly- this can include pleasant or unpleasant feelings. After the free write is over, ask students how the activity made them feel and how it might function as a positive coping habit. Encourage them to share their free write with a trusted adult if they want or even to tear it up if they want to move on from a negative issue.

## Move It

Teach the class how to communicate their feelings through movement. For example, you might model tiptoeing around the room to show nervousness or jumping up and down in excitement. Have the class brainstorm various classroom-appropriate movements for different feelings and chart their ideas. Then let everyone express a feeling through movement at the same time. Finally ask if any volunteers want to "perform" their expressive movements for the class. Process this activity by discussing what parts of the activity that students found helpful and/or uncomfortable.

## Feelings Sculptures

Pair up students and give each pair some clay. Have the pairs shape the clay to show something that has been difficult for them this week, then flatten their clay difficulty, and then shape the clay to show an action that helped them feel better during their difficult time. Each student in the pair should have a turn to do this. Ask students to tell how they felt while watching their partner shape their difficulty and then their helping action.

## My Picture of Success

Have students fold a piece of paper in half. On one side of the paper, they should draw and color a picture of a school success that they have experienced in their life. One the other side of the paper they should write 3 words or phrases to explain how they were able to be successful during this time. Organize the class into groups to share their successes and process the activity. Consider adding a gallery walk so that everyone can see each other's successes.

## Body Breaths

Teach the class a breathing activity that involves focusing on body movements to center one's self. Have them take a deep breath in, imagining their lungs filling with air. Then they can exhale while imaging their lungs deflating as the air leaves them. Next have them breathe in while raising their arms above their heads and breathe out while lowering their arms. Repeat 2 more times. Process the activity with a few questions to the class about how they liked, disliked, or experienced the breath work.

# CONCLUSION

## Hope for the Future

One of the biggest issues in working with struggling and traumatized students is that there is little time to reflect on the helping process because counselors are so busy actually doing the helping. This reflection is crucial for making systemic changes needed to solve the root problems causing the trauma. Fortunately, using this book automatically creates a change in systems for your hardest hit students. Putting a plan into place that teaches every child how to interrupt child abuse, get help in a crisis, experience academic success, and use positive coping habits, is a game-changer! A plan of this nature moves the needle because it creates an environment where everyone is less negatively affected by life's difficulties. This, in turn, begins to break the trauma cycle- if we teach our students how to be safer, happier, and more successful, they will eventually grow into adults who can pass this knowledge and lifestyle onto the next generation.

## Next Steps

But where do we go from here? What is our next step? How about changing social systems and institutions that expose children to traumatic events? Even well-meaning institutions such as schools, the foster care system, and juvenile justice, can contribute to grooming practices and inequitable environments that expose children to trauma (Henfield, et al., 2019). It is time for conversations and actions to occur at a mainstream level in order to analyze the systems that contribute to childhood trauma. The call-to-action then becomes working collectively in schools and communities to mount a large-scale response; this response must interrupt systems that oppress and terrorize marginalized children. The time has come to gather our courage and work together to name and fix various systems that need to change (Goldin & Khasnabis, 2020). Together we can disrupt systems and practices that harm children. This is the next big frontier in trauma-informed practices and we are up for the challenge.

## Thank You

You now have everything you need to incorporate trauma-informed practices into your school counseling with students. Whether your children have suffered a traumatic experience or are just dealing with the day-to-day challenges of life, you've got them covered! Before I sign off and wrap up this whole adventure, I want to take a moment to tell you that your work is making such a difference in the lives of children, especially the traumatized ones. Unfortunately, we do not get to hear that enough in our profession, because we are in the business of solving problems. This means that we hear a lot about problems, but we don't usually get to hear about the solutions of our time spent counseling. Let me be the one to tell you that what you are doing matters so, so much. On behalf of all the children whose lives you are changing... ***Thank you***.

# References

*If you would like to learn more about any of the strategies or activities in this counseling guide, please refer to the sources below.*


American School Counselor Association. (2019). *The ASCA National Model 4th Ed*. Alexandria, VA: author.

American School Counselor Association. (2018). *The school counselor and multitiered system of supports*. Retrieved from https://www.schoolcounselor.org/asca/media/asca/PositionStatements/PS_MTSS.pdf

American School Counselor Association. (2016). *The school counselor and trauma-informed practice*. Retrieved from https://www.schoolcounselor.org/asca/media/asca/PositionStatements/PS_TraumaInformed.pdf

American Society for the Positive Care of Children. (2018). *National child abuse statistics*. Retrieved from https://americanspcc.org/child-abuse-statistics/

Burke, N. (2018). *The deepest well: Healing the long-term effects of childhood adversity*. New York, NY: Houghton Mifflin Harcourt Publishing Company.

Centers for Disease Control and Prevention. (2019). *About adverse childhood experiences*. Retrieved from https://www.cdc.gov/violenceprevention/acestudy/about_ace.html

Centers for Disease Control and Prevention. (n.d). *Coping with a traumatic event*. Retrieved from https://www.cdc.gov/masstrauma/factsheets/public/coping.pdf

Centers for Disease Control and Prevention. (2009). *School connectedness: Strategies for increasing protective factors among youth*. Retrieved from https://www.cdc.gov/healthyyouth/protective/pdf/connectness.pdf

Cleveland Clinic. (2015). *Stressed out? Aromatherapy can help you feel calmer.* Retrieved from https://health.clevelandclinic.org/stressed-out-aromatherapy-can-help-you-to-feel-calmer/

College Board. (2020). *Learn more, earn more*. Retrieved from https://bigfuture.collegeboard.org/get-started/know-yourself/learn-more-earn-more

Corey, M., Corey., G., & Corey, C. (2017). *Groups process and practice 10th ed*. Boston, MA: Cengage Learning.

De Shazer, S. (1988). *Clues: Investigating solutions in brief therapy*. New York: Norton.

Goldin, S. & Khasnabis, D. (2020). Trauma-informed practice is a powerful tool, but it's also incomplete. *Education Week*. Retrieved from https://www.edweek.org/ew/articles/2020/02/20/trauma-informed-practice-is-a-powerful-tool-but.html

Hubbs Ullman, K. (2004). *Group Interventions for Treatment of Psychological Trauma Module One*. Retrieved from https://www.agpa.org/docs/default-source/practice-resources/group-interventions-for-treatment-of-trauma-in-adults.pdf?sfvrsn=8f6985a9_2

Henfield, M., Washington, A.R., Bersevic, Z. et al. Introduction to Trauma-Informed Practices for Mental Health and Wellness in Urban Schools and Communities. Urban Rev 51, 537–539 (2019). https://doi.org/10.1007/s11256-019-00541-2

Kaffenberger, C. (2013). *Making data work*. Alexandria, VA: American School Counselor Association.

Kidshealth.com. (2019). *Making a change in your life.* Retrieved from https://kidshealth.org/en/teens/make-change.html

Lee, Y., Park, B., and Kim, S. (2011). The effects of heat and massage application on autonomic nervous system. *Yonsei Medical Journal.* Retrieved from https://www.ncbi.nlm.nih.gov/pmc/articles/PMC3220246/

Lerner, S. (2018). *Get your group on volume one*. South Carolina: Youthlight, www.youthlight.com.

Lerner, S. (2018). *Get Your group on volume two*. South Carolina: Youthlight, www.youthlight.com.

Lutz, A. (2018). *Helping clients heal from trauma: Solution focused approach*. Retrieved from https://solutionfocused.net/2018/07/05/helping-clients-heal-from-trauma-solution-focused-approach/

Milne, A.A. (1926). *Winnie-the-Pooh*. New York: Dutton & Co.

Morin, A. (2015.) *Seven scientifically proven benefits of gratitude*. Retrieved from: https://www.psychologytoday.com/us/blog/what-mentally-strong-people-dont-do/201504/7-scientifically-proven-benefits-gratitude

National Association of School Psychologists. (2015). *Recommended books for children coping with loss or trauma*. Retrieved from https://www.nasponline.org/x33507.xml

National Institute for the Clinical Application of Behavioral Medicine. (2017). *How trauma can impact four types of memory*. [Infographic]. Retrieved from https://www.nicabm.com/trauma-how-trauma-can-impact-4-types-of-memory-infographic/

National Institute of Mental Health. (2017). *Coping with traumatic events*. Retrieved from https://www.nimh.nih.gov/health/topics/coping-with-traumatic-events/index.shtml

NCTSN Core Curriculum on Childhood Trauma Task Force (2012). *The 12 core concepts: Concepts for understanding traumatic stress responses in children and families*. Core Curriculum on Childhood Trauma. Los Angeles, CA, and Durham, NC: UCLA Duke University National Center for Child Traumatic Stress.

Neff, K. (2020). *The chemicals of care: How self-compassion manifests in our bodies*. Retrieved from https://self-compassion.org/the-chemicals-of-care-how-self-compassion-manifests-in-our-bodies/

Nike. (2006). *Failure*. Retrieved from https://www.youtube.com/watch?v=45mMioJ5szc

Pendarvis, S. & Shook, J. (2017). Educate to prevent child abuse. *ASCA School Counselor*, 64 (3), 32-35.

Perry, B & Szalavitz, M. (2017). *The boy who was raised as a dog*. New York: Basic Books.

Karyn B. Purvis, David R. Cross, Donald F. Dansereau & Sheri R. Parris (2013) Trust-Based Relational Intervention (TBRI): A Systemic Approach to Complex Developmental Trauma, Child & Youth Services, 34:4, 360-386, DOI: 10.1080/0145935X.2013.859906

Sabella, R. (2019). *The solution focused brief approach: From problem solver to solution seeker*. Retrieved from http://bit.ly/sfbc-packet

Silverstein, S. (1974). *Where the sidewalk ends*. New York: Harper & Row Publishers, Inc.

Sklare, G. (2014). *Brief counseling that works. 3rd edition*. California: Corwin Press.

Sobhy, M., & Cavallaro, M. (2010). *Solution-focused brief counseling in schools: Theoretical perspectives and case application to an elementary school student*. Retrieved from http://counselingoutfitters.com/vistas/vistas10/Article_81.pdf

Youth.gov. (2020). *Risk and protective factors*. Retrieved from https://youth.gov/youth-topics/youth-mental-health/risk-and-protective-factors-youth

# ABOUT THE AUTHOR

Stephanie Lerner is a Johns Hopkins University-trained school counselor. She holds a BS in elementary education and an MS in counseling. With more than 20 years in both public and private education, she has Texas certifications in school counseling and bilingual/Spanish education. After traveling the world and teaching in such far off places as Mozambique and Bolivia, Stephanie came home to the United States to be a bilingual counselor and teacher in a high-need public school system. When she's not writing or educating, she enjoys ranch life with her husband and their menagerie of pets—all of whom practice healthy coping skills, of course!

**For any questions you have related to this book, direct them to Stephanie Lerner at schoolcounselorstephanie.com.**

**Like her Facebook page and follow her on Instagram or Pinterest to receive info about her other upcoming books.**

www.schoolcounselorstephanie.com
www.facebook.com/schoolcounselorstephanie
www.instagram.com/schoolcounselorstephanie
www.pinterest.com/schoolcounselorstephanie